LOST ARIZONA TREASURE

LOST ARIZONA TREASURE

W. CRAIG GAINES

THE History PRESS

Published by The History Press
An imprint of Arcadia Publishing
Charleston, SC
www.historypress.com

First published 2025

Manufactured in the United States

ISBN 9781467159319

Library of Congress Control Number: 2025931937

CONTENTS

INTRODUCTION

Arizona became a state in 1912 after many centuries of conflict between American Indians and colonization efforts by Spain, Mexico and the United States. The Apaches, Pimas (Akimei O'odhams), Papagos (Tohono O'oldhams), Yumas (Quechans) and other Indian tribes resisted colonization and forced removal from their lands. Arizona was part of American Indian, Spanish, Mexican and American lands and has the legends and stories to prove it. Most legends come from enhancements of actual historical events. I have added history and other information to these stories of lost Arizona treasure.

I lived in Tucson and traveled throughout Arizona. The legends and stories in this book were collected over many years. I started collecting treasure stories when I was in junior high school when I got my first metal detector. I've also had a lifelong interest in geology and minerals.

Arizona is the home of many lost mine stories. The world-famous Lost Dutchman Mine is the best known of these lost mines. The Lost Adams Diggings is another famous lost Arizona mine. Both of these may have been found and mined out.

The Spanish explored what is now Arizona in search of gold and silver deposits similar to what they found in Mexico. The Spaniards found huge copper deposits that they eventually mined along with gold and silver. The Spanish established presidios, towns and missions in Arizona. Arizona became part of the new independent nation of Mexico when it broke away from Spain. Arizona became American when Mexico lost the Mexican-American War and signed the Treaty of Guadalupe Hidalgo.

When the California Gold Rush started in 1849 and the Gadsden Purchase was completed in 1854, thousands of prospectors entered Arizona. Tales of lost Spanish mines in the mountains and washes coming off the mountains caused many to look for these mines. Some prospectors going to and coming from the California gold fields discovered Arizona gold and silver deposits. Hostile Apache and other tribal raids caused many mines to be abandoned or lost when the miners were killed or chased away.

U.S. Army forts and outposts were established during the Indian Wars, which resulted in the Indian tribes decimated and often confined to reservations. Tales of lost mines are everywhere in Arizona, especially from periods of hostile Indian outbreaks. Finally, Arizona Territory became civilized, and the Indian Wars ended. Arizona is part of the legacy of the Old West.

Newspapers and magazines published many lost treasure and lost mine stories, as readers were interested in reading about and finding lost wealth for themselves, especially during times of economic depression. Values and potential values of lost treasures in this book are based on what other writers have noted. Often these values are unreasonable. J. Frank Dobie, Thomas Penfield, Robert Marx, W.C. Jameson and Thomas P. Terry gathered many treasure-trove and lost mine stories in their books. Prolific writer Maurice Kildare (the pen name of Gladwell "Toney" Richardson) wrote original lost treasure stories from his years working in American Indian trading posts in Arizona. With metal detecting becoming a hobby in the late 1960s, many treasure and Old West–focused magazines published lost treasure and lost mines stories.

I have tried to briefly present each legend, story and history based on my research, analysis and understanding. Many lost treasures and lost mines have extensive write-ups in books and articles. Where a tale covers more than one county, I noted it and have separate entries by county. Where possible, several stories or versions of stories have been consolidated. Some tales have been retold so many times that there are a number of different accounts with multiple locations and different names for the participants. I attempted to sort through a lot of information and present it in a logical sequence. Errors of interpretation and information are likely. These stories are often based on oral traditions that were written down after being retold multiple times over many years. Where stories have been proven to be fraudulent, I have stated so based on historical research. At times, the production of fake treasure maps was a cottage industry, so some tales likely involved fake maps to hunt for treasure that didn't exist. Some lost mines were marketing tales by prospectors looking for a grubstake so they could continue looking for the big strike that would make them rich.

Many areas with lost treasures and lost mines lore in Arizona are parts of protected lands—national parks, national forests, Bureau of Land Management lands, state parks, local parks and so on. Some Arizona lands are in private ownership. Valid mining claims exist in many areas that have lost mine stories. Arizona has much beautiful and unique scenery that welcomes the visitor, so I hope you can visit and enjoy the magnificent Arizona scenery as you go down its trails. Don't forget to keep a sharp lookout for lost treasure and lost mines.

1896 Arizona Territory map. *New York Public Library.*

ARIZONA TREASURES BY COUNTY

Apache County

Lost Adams Diggings
See Graham County.

Lost Black Burro Mine
See Navajo County.

Lost Carson Mine
Jim Carson was a freighter who carried goods between Fort Defiance and Camp Verde in 1875. He and his Mexican employee reportedly camped at Pueblo Colorado Wash near Ganado, on the Navajo Reservation. A mule left his camp that night. Jim Carson went out alone to recover the mule. His Mexican teamster drove the freight wagon the next morning down the road as Carson believed that he would quickly find the mule.

Carson found the mule about a mile away from where they had camped. On his way back to the camp, he found a gully full of black sand peppered with shiny gold flakes. Carson erected a pole at the placer gold deposit to mark the location, which was near a spring. He rejoined his freight wagon with some of the gold he picked up.

Jim Carson returned to the placer gold deposit and recovered $2,500 worth of gold. He went to Fort Defiance and got a partner, Jack Williams,

Left: The chief of the Yavapai Apaches at Camp Verde. Hostile tribes caused many mines to be abandoned and lost. *Library of Congress.*

Below: Fort Defiance was one of many U.S. Army forts established to protect settlers and miners from hostile Indians. *Library of Congress.*

who was a trader near the fort. Carson gave Williams directions to the placer mine he discovered. Williams agreed to go there and build a cabin. Jim Carson headed for California to get his brother to help with the mining. Jim Carson was killed by Apaches before he could reach California. Williams searched in vain for about a year for the placer deposit. Some believe that this lost mine is still unfound.

LOST NAVAJO SILVER MINE
Rumored to be near Dennehotso.

LOST REINA DE ESPANA MINE
Supposedly near the Canyon de Chelly National Monument.

LOST SHOEMAKER MINE
Said to be in Apache County.

LOST SILVER MONUMENT VALLEY MINE
See Navajo County.

COCHISE COUNTY

ALVORD-STILES GANG LOOT
In 1899, three masked men robbed the Southern Pacific Express Train at the watering station of Cochise. Cochise was about eleven miles west of Wilcox and four miles from the site of an 1895 train robbery. See Train Robbery Coins.

Wilcox Constable Burt Alvord and his deputies William N. "Billy" Stiles and Bob Downing led posses looking for the outlaws. It turns out that Alvord, Stiles and Downing were all part of the outlaw Alvord-Stile Gang, which reportedly robbed the train and hid caches near Pearce. One of these caches was reportedly $60,000 in gold bullion and coins (or $80,000 in gold bullion) hidden in the Dos Cabezas Mountains. Some caches have been reportedly found in the area. The Alvord-Stiles Gang was headquartered Pearce for a time.

Wells Fargo agent John Thacker investigated the robbery and discovered that Bob Downing had been spending new ten-dollar gold coins. Thacker learned that Alvord was involved with the outlaw gang that robbed the

The Cochise County desert and mountains hide many lost treasures and lost mines. *New York Public Library.*

train. Alvord left his post as sheriff in December 1899. He reportedly had a gambling and drinking problem. Stiles and Alvord were captured by the law several times but escaped each time in 1901 and 1903. Finally, the Arizona Rangers captured Alvord in Mexico. He spent two years in the Yuma Territorial Prison. After his release from prison, Alvord left for Central America in 1910, where he worked on the Panama Canal and disappeared.

Bags of Gold

Outlaws reportedly hid two bags of gold about thirty miles northwest of Douglas near an old camp.

Big House Treasure

This treasure, said to have been $115,000 in gold coins, was hidden at Charleston.

Black Jack Ketchum Treasure

Outlaw "Black Jack" Thomas Edward Ketchum reportedly hid his loot in a cave in Wildcat Canyon in the Chiricahua Mountains. Leonard Alvorsen, a gang member, was in the Yuma Territorial Prison when he claimed that his gang had hidden the treasure in a cave they called Room Forty-Four. Black Jack Ketchum supposedly told Sheriff Cicero Stuart about the gang's hidden loot while he was in jail. Stuart later led a search team to Wildcat Canyon. They found nothing. One version of this story was that Ketchum had set the sheriff up for an ambush to kill the lawman. Black Jack Ketchum was hanged in 1901 for attempted train robbery in Union County, New Mexico Territory. Ketchum was once part of the Hole in the Wall Gang.

Can Can Treasures

A flood in Tombstone washed away gold and silver coins in the Can Can Restaurant (or Saloon) at Fourth Street and Allen Street, which were not known to have been recovered. This restaurant was founded in 1879. Many different businesses have been at this location.

Another tale claimed an employee from the Can Can stole money and went to prison for the crime. While in prison, he claimed that he buried the money in the Boot Hill Graveyard (or Old Cemetery) at various sites that were dug up, but no money was ever found. The thief died after a short time in jail.

Charleston Caches

Several caches were rumored to have been hidden in the ghost town of Charleston, which is about eight miles southwest of Tombstone. One story has the Cowboys Gang outlaws Zwing Hunt and Billy Grounds and possibly other outlaws robbing the Tombstone Mining and Milling Company in Charleston of bullion. The outlaws supposedly took the bullion and hid it before being killed or fleeing the area. Several caches have been reportedly found in the area. The Charleston area was a base for outlaws who robbed Mexican mule trains in Skeleton Canyon. See Skeleton Canyon Treasure, Big House Treasure and Zwing Hunt's Davis Mountain Treasure.

Colt's Cache

The first commander of Fort Bowie, Theodore Colt, supposedly received kickbacks that he hid in 1863 near Apache Pass.

Earp Brothers Treasure

The Earp brothers were said to have hidden a cache in Tombstone when they ran the town. Since all the Earp brothers but Morgan Earp survived their encounters with the Cowboys Gang, there is likely no lost Earp brothers treasure.

Fort Bowie guarded Apache Pass, which was the scene of many battles. *Library of Congress.*

Fort Huachuca Treasure

A legend claimed that Mexican outlaw Juan Estrada hid two sacks containing fifty pounds each of gold bullion in Huachuca Canyon not far from Fort Huachuca. U.S. Army soldier Robert Jones claimed in 1941 that he found stacked treasure when he fell into a deep hole in Huachuca Canyon. He returned to the site with a flashlight. He said he found stacked gold and silver ingots, a wood box with gold nuggets inside and box half full of gold dust. Jones also claimed that he found a bottle with a document in Spanish inside. He scraped off some gold and later sold it. He and his friend Sam Mays reportedly covered the shaft to the treasure. Sam Mays was killed in action during World War II in Italy. Jones was severely wounded in the South Pacific. It took several years for Jones to recover.

In 1959, Jones searched for the cache with heavy equipment but never found any treasure. The shaft was filled with water; the tunnel had caved in and was hard to find after several digging attempts. Jones died in 1968. In 1975, California treasure hunting company Quest Exploration used sensors to hunt for cavities in the ground at the site. It gave up searching. The U.S. Army was rumored to have done excavation at the site with bulldozers in 1979. Fort Huachuca is now the site of the vast U.S. Army proving grounds.

Lost Fortune (Fortuna) Mine
See Pima County.

Lost Shepard's Mine
Rumored to be in southern Cochise County.

Lost Skeleton Mine
Said to be in Skeleton Canyon in the Peloncillo Mountains.

Lost Virgin Guadalupe Mine/Lost Mine of the Guadalupes
Possibly somewhere in Cochise County.

Rincon Mountains Lost Treasure
A cache of gold bullion and gold dust was said to have been stashed in a cave near Benson and the Buckhorn Ranch, about sixty miles from Mexico.

Ruster's Park Caches
Several caches of coins, gold dust and bullion were rumored to be in the Rustler's Park area not far from Paradise, Galeyville and Sunglow.

Sandstone Lost Mine
Said to be somewhere in Cochise County.

Skeleton Canyon Treasure

Skeleton Canyon is in the Peloncillo Mountains and connects the Animas Valley, New Mexico, with the San Simon Valley (or San Bernardino Valley), Arizona. It is near the Mexican border and San Luis Pass. It got its name from the skeletons of men, burros and horses found there over the years. It is part of the Smuggler's Trail, which connected Tucson to Sonora. An Anglo-American outlaw gang called the Cowboys used the communities of Charleston and Galeyville as their bases to raid the Smuggler's Trail, the surrounding area and northern Mexico.

In 1879, about half a mile from the mouth of Skeleton Canyon, Mexican smugglers were said to have been attacked by the Cowboys, consisting of "Old Man" Ike Clanton, Billy Clanton, Frank McLowery, Tom McLowery, Jim Hughes, Zwing Hunt, Billy Grounds, Charlie Thomas, Charlie Snow and other outlaws. This first robbery reportedly killed nineteen Mexicans, with only a small boy escaping.

Another version of this first Skeleton Canyon story was that the Cowboys had just raided Mexican ranches in northern Sonora. Mexican Captain Alfredo Carrillo led a detachment of *rurales* after the outlaw gang but was ambushed in Skeleton Canyon by the outlaws. Only three of the *rurales* were said to have escaped the ambush.

In July 1881, the gang—then consisting of "Old Man" Ike Clanton, Billy Clanton, Jack McKenzie, Zwing Hunt, Billy Grounds and another outlaw—ambushed a Mexican smuggling train near where the 1879 ambush previously occurred. At least six smugglers were killed. The thirty to forty mules carrying a treasure reportedly consisting of $90,000 in Mexican silver dollars and thirty-nine gold bars scattered and had to be hunted down by the outlaws. Some of the packs may have broken and their contents scattered on the ground. The outlaws had to kill some burros to get the treasure the burros carried.

Zwing Hunt was wounded in the shoulder during the attack. This small outlaw band reportedly did not have enough horses and burros to transport both them and the treasure. They were said to have buried part of the gold and silver below a grouping of three old oak trees.

While most of the outlaws were celebrating at Galeyville, Zwing Hunt and Billy Grounds dug up the hidden treasure and put it in a wagon. They murdered the wagon driver and burned the wagon after they hid this treasure. Hunt and Grounds reportedly stayed at a nearby cabin while Hunt recovered from his wound. They may have stopped at Jack Chandler's Ranch near Charleston.

Another probably more factual story was that the July 1881 attack on the Mexican party was executed by Curley Bill Brocious, Johnny Ringo, Jim Crane and about twenty other outlaws. This version had four Mexicans killed with $2,500 in gold and silver coins, livestock and mescal stolen by the gang. Some stories claimed that the treasure was worth $3 million.

Rurales led again by Captain Alfredo Carrillo were said to have ambushed some of the Cowboys Gang in Guadalupe Canyon in the Peloncillo Mountains on August 13, 1881. The *rurales* killed five outlaws, including "Old Man" Ike Clanton. Other versions of this story have Wyatt Earp and two of his brothers killing Ike Clanton, Charlie Snow, Jim Crane, Dick Gray and Billy Lane.

Zwing Hunt, Billy Grounds and possibly other outlaws attempted to rob an ore stamp mill at Charleston. A posse went after these outlaws for the robbery attempt. Another story claimed that the posse was after them for cattle rustling. Billy Grounds and Zwing Hunt got into a gun battle the next day with Tombstone Sheriff Billy Breckinridge and the posse. Billy Grounds died during the fight, and Zwing Hunt was badly wounded and hospitalized in Tombstone. Zwing Hunt's brother came to Tombstone and helped Zwing escape. While the Hunts were camped out hiding, a band of Indians reportedly attacked them and killed Zwing. His brother escaped.

This outlaw gang reportedly hid their loot in Skeleton Canyon in the Chiricahua Mountains. Some tales claimed that Zwing Hunt escaped death and hid his treasure on Davis Mountain before dying. His half-brother Hugh Davis reportedly spent thirty years looking for his brother's caches.

Thirty years later, a $5,000 treasure was reportedly found at the cabin where Zwing Hunt and Billy Grounds had stayed after the 1881 Skeleton Canyon robbery. Dobie Mexican dollars have reportedly also been found in the area of the attacks. A rotted rawhide bag with $2,000 in Mexican Dobie dollars was supposedly found in the area by a cowboy and government official.

J. Bellow's article "Ghosts Guard the Gold" appeared in *True Treasure* and *Lost Treasure* magazines. This article discussed his search with his wife and friends in Skeleton Canyon and the recovery of four Mexican Dobie dollars dated between 1864 and 1880 and a spent .45-.70 rifle cartridge casing. See Zwing Hunt's Davis Mountain Treasure.

Train Robbery Coins

On June 30, 1895, cowboys turned outlaws Grant Wheeler and Joe Georges boarded a Southern Pacific Railroad train in Wilcox and later forced the engineer to halt the train about four miles west of Wilcox. The robbers detached all the cars behind the express car and forced the train engineer to drive the train down the track. Unbeknownst to the robbers, the expressman moved many valuables from the express car to the passenger cars that were left behind. The outlaws forced the engineer to halt the train about eight miles west of Wilcox, where the outlaws had their horses and a supply of dynamite. Georges got the horses and dynamite, while Wheeler forced the engineer and fireman to break into the express car.

Inside the express car, they found eight sacks of Mexican Dobie dollars, with each sack containing one thousand coins. They also found a locked safe. Using the dynamite, they set explosives off three times to open the safe. They used several sacks of the Mexican coins to hold the dynamite close to the safe. The dynamite explosions finally blew open the express car doors, scattering silver dollars around the express car for a long distance. There was little of value in the safe. Wheeler and Georges put sacks of coins on their horses and fled. Wheeler was later cornered by railroad agents and reportedly committed suicide. Georges disappeared and was never caught.

The railroad had their men gather what loose coins they could find from the robbery. It was thought that about eight thousand coins had been blown out of the express car and scattered about. Afterward, people combed the area with hoes trying to unearth scattered coins. It is thought that a few coins may have been missed. About seven thousand coins were thought to have been recovered. Undoubtedly, people with metal detectors have searched the area for lost coins in recent years. This was about four miles from a later 1899 robbery site by the Alvord-Stiles Gang. See Alvord-Stiles Gang Loot.

Wagon Train Cache

Apaches were said to have taken gold dust and silver coins from a wagon train a few miles northeast of the Mountain Springs Stage Station. The loot was reportedly put in a Dutch oven and stashed been two rocks in the Winchester Mountains northeast of Wilcox. This could be in Graham County.

Wells Fargo Loot

Chief Cochise was a mighty warrior whose band attacked ranches, wagon trains and stagecoaches. Chief Cochise and his Chiricahua Apaches reportedly cached two Wells Fargo chests containing gold coins from an attack on stagecoaches. One location was said to have been in a cave near Dragoon Pass. Cochise's stronghold was in the Dragoon Mountains, possibly in Stronghold Canyon (or China Meadow). Cochise signed a treaty with the

United States on October 12, 1872, and spent his remaining days on the Chiricahua Apache reservation.

Zwing Hunt's Davis Mountains Treasure

According to one tale, Zwing Hunt may have escaped death after being attacked by Indians but was severely wounded. Hunt returned home to San Antonio, Texas, and died there from his injuries. Before dying, Zwing Hunt gave his uncle a map with instructions to his treasure cache. The cache was reportedly buried at the base of Davis Mountain and could be in New Mexico. The name Davis Mountain was the name Zwing Hunt gave the mountain. The exact site of the mountain was not clear. This could be in the Peloncillo Mountains. A grave was said to be at the base of this mountain. See Skeleton Canyon Treasure.

Coconino County

Baking Soda Treasure

A cache of $2,000 in gold (or $15,000) from the sale of Sam Clevenger's cattle was reportedly hidden in a baking soda can on the Colorado River near Lee's Ferry. Sam Clevenger, his wife and their daughter, Jessie Clevenger, left Stafford, Arizona, bound to start a new life elsewhere. They had a wagon full of their possessions, about one hundred horses and two cowboys to assist them on their journey. The cowboys were called Wilson and Johnson. Mrs. Clevenger hid the baking soda tin in the stove in their wagon while traveling. Each night, she buried the baking soda tin near where they camped. Only she knew where it was hidden. The Clevengers, the two cowboys and the horses arrived at Lee's Ferry at dusk and spent the night in a grove of pine trees several hundred yards off the main road.

The next morning, Wilson and Johnson murdered Sam Clevenger and his wife with an axe. Their daughter, Jessie Clevenger, claimed that she was captured by Wilson and Johnson as she tried to hide nearby. The cowboys searched for the baking soda tin in the wagon, but it wasn't there. Then they searched the area and were unable to find it. The cowboys burned the wagon and its contents. They buried their two victims, took Jessie Clevenger and the herd of horses and headed north.

Travelers discovered the graves and the burned wagon. The sheriff of Prescott and a posse went after the murderers. The posse followed their trail as they sold off horses for money along their way. The sheriff captured Wilson and Jessie Clevenger in Idaho and later caught Johnson in Montana. They were taken to Prescott, where Wilson and Johnson were tried for murder. Jessie Clevenger was questioned and released. Wilson was hanged for the murders. Johnson was sent to prison but was later released. Jessie Clevenger led parties to search for the buried treasure. The sheriff also hunted for the treasure. Eventually, Jessie Clevenger married. It was believed that the treasure existed near Lee's Ferry. In 1887, $2,000 in gold would probably be worth $200,000 today. The question I have is whether $2,000 in gold would fit into just one baking soda tin.

Brown's Outlaw Cache

Louis "Louie the Hermit" Brown was a miner and an outlaw in hiding. He supposedly cached $150,000 in silver and gold coins several places after he and his gang robbed a train near Tucson. He double-crossed his outlaw partners and ran off with all the loot. His partners finally caught up with him and killed him. His murderers reportedly recovered some of the loot, but not all of it. The caches were said to be somewhere in the Grand Canyon National Park.

Canyon Diablo Treasure

A cache of gold coins was hidden in Canyon Diablo according to some sources.

Grand Canyon Waterfall Cache and Lost Mine

Prospector Long Tom Watson found an unopened letter in a box of unopened mail and catalogues in an abandoned shack on the edge of Flagstaff in late November 1910. Watson was spending the winter there and finally opened one of the letters in January 1911; it turned out to be a letter from a dying prospector to his brother. The letter said that the prospector had found a rich placer deposit in the Grand Canyon area and was visited by two suspicious men. He threw a bag full of gold nuggets under a nearby waterfall. When he returned to his camp where the two men were, he got into a gunfight with them and was severely wounded. He shot one of the men, and they both left. He barely made it back to civilization and was dying under a doctor's care when he wrote the letter, dated March 28, 1904, and mailed it with directions to the gold cache and lost mine.

Several lost mine stories are based in the Grand Canyon area. *Library of Congress.*

Long Tom Watson searched for the treasure from 1911 to June 1914, when he heard the sound of water and found a twenty-two-foot-high waterfall east of Havasupai Canyon that matched the location on the map. From the top of the waterfall, he saw a cave behind it fifteen feet below him. He jumped into the cave and found gold nuggets scattered about. He stuffed the largest gold nuggets in his pockets and tried to climb up the slippery walls to the top of the cliff but couldn't. He fell back into the pool below the waterfall and broke his leg. There was placer gold in the pool and stream. With much effort, he managed to reach his horse and burro and made it to the Martin Buggelin Ranch on the south side of the Grand Canyon. He was taken to Flagstaff, where it took months for him to recover from his leg infection.

He searched several years for the waterfall, but it was a seasonal waterfall, so the pool and stream were dry most of the time. He and his friend, veterinarian Doc Scanlon, looked for the waterfall but never found it. Eventually, Watson became depressed and committed suicide.

Lost Coconino Mine

Said to be about twenty miles southwest of Flagstaff in the southwestern part of the county. Another rumored location was northeast of Desert View, near the Grand Canyon, the Colorado River and the Little Colorado River.

Lost Deadman Mine

May be southwest of Cameron.

Lost Jackass Dobson Mine and Treasure

A lost mine and cache of gold bullion was rumored to be in the Flagstaff area.

Lost John D. Lee Mines and Treasure

John D. Lee had 19 wives and 56 children. Lee was a founding member of the Latter-day Saints. He was a key member of the Mormons and took part in the Mountain Meadows massacre in September 1857. The Baker-Fancher Party from Arkansas was heading for California but was attacked and murdered by Mormon militia and their Paiute Indian allies. The attack took place because the Mormons believed that members of the wagon train had been responsible for the murder of Mormons in the Haun's Mill Massacre on October 30, 1838, in Caldwell County, Missouri, when 17 Mormons were murdered. About 120 people in the Baker-Fancher Party were killed.

Lee was said to have found and mined placer gold and maybe lode gold at a secret location. There could have been more than one mine location since both placer gold and lode gold are mentioned in his lost mine stories. Some thought that he buried seven cans of recovered placer gold somewhere. He was arrested in 1874 and tried twice. The second trial in 1876 convicted him of murder. While he was under arrest, he wrote a letter to one of his daughters talking about his gold ledge. He was executed on March 23, 1877, by a firing squad at the site of the Mountain Meadows Massacre. John D. Lee was the only Mormon executed for the murders at this massacre. Lee claimed that he was a scapegoat and had been railroaded by other guilty Mormons like Bishop Isaac C. Haight (who went by the alias of Brown) and Jacob Hamlin.

John D. Lee's lost mines are in the Grand Canyon area. *New York Public Library.*

The placer mine was reportedly in the Grand Canyon area in a canyon above the Vulture's Throne, which is on the north side of the Colorado River some six miles southeast of Mount Emma. Other potential locations were near Lee's Ferry, Lee's Farm and the Navajo Bridge. The area where the lost mine is thought to be located is the Grand Canyon National Park, the Navajo Nation or the Kaibab National Forest.

One of John D. Lee's defense attorneys, Judge Wells Spier, questioned Lee's family about his mine and searched for it. Robert B. Hildebrand was part of Lee's group when he was a young boy. Hildebrand recalled later in life that he accompanied John Lee on some of his mining trips and always was left in a camp while Lee went to his mine. When Lee returned, he would have tin cans filled with gold nuggets carried by packhorses. Hildebrand's last trip with John Lee was said to have been fifty-five miles west from Lee's Ferry along the canyon rim to a wasteland area.

It is hard to believe that any of John D. Lee's vast family did not know the location of his gold mine. His wife, Emma, who ran the ferry business at Lee's Ferry, was said to have had a map to his mine. After Lee's execution, Emma lived in Holbrook and reportedly took gold and silver with her from the ferry—possibly as much as $7,000. Emma married rancher Franklin French. Emma supplied the money for her new husband to expand irrigation projects in Lower Creek Canyon. Emma provided her new husband information on John D. Lee's lost mine. Franklin French searched repeatedly without success for John D. Lee's lost mine. Maurice Kildare's article on the Lost John D. Lee Mines had a lot of research behind it.

Lost Morgan Mine
Supposedly a four-hour trek south of Flagstaff.

Lost Padre Mine
May have been in Coconino County.

Lost Silver Mine of Sierra Azul
Said to be in the San Francisco Peaks region.

Lost Teller Mine
The Havasupai Indians were said to have had a silver mine on the flank of Elder Mountain northeast of Flagstaff. From this mine, they reportedly got silver that they made into jewelry. Teller was a prospector who hunted for this mine and was said to have found it. His body was found with a rich sack of silver ore next to it. Indians, outlaws or a fellow prospector were thought to have killed him. People searched for his mine, but no one has claimed to have found it.

Lost Tonto Apache Mine
Supposedly, it was within a two-hour walk of Sedona. This could be in Yavapai County.

The San Francisco Mountains reportedly guard a lost silver mine and lost treasure. *New York Public Library.*

Lost Treasure of the Padres

A legend claimed that padres cached a treasure in the San Francisco Peaks area, north of Flagstaff.

Mercury Cache

A stash of mercury worth about $65,000 was reportedly hidden near Lee's Ferry.

Nelson's Lost Loot

Near Stoneman Lake, a cache of loot consisting of several thousand dollars may have been hidden by robbers Earl Nelson and a man called Forrester. Nelson and Forrester robbed a Clarkdale bank in June 1928. Forrester was later killed. Nelson was captured by the law and sent to prison. It was believed that neither robber ever recovered their loot.

Mormon Mountain Lost Mine and Treasure

This lost mine and a cache of gold and silver coins were said to have been stashed near Mormon Lake.

Pine Springs Treasure

Pine Springs was a stage station on the Star Stage Line between Prescott and Santa Fe, New Mexico. It was in the Coconino National Forest off National Forest Road no. 22 near Mahan Mountain. In 1879, four robbers reportedly attacked a stagecoach drawn by six horses near the stage stop and stole three boxes of uncirculated gold coins said to have been worth $225,000. The passenger on the stagecoach was killed in the robbery. The stage driver, Mose Stacey, escaped and ran into a nearby posse. The four outlaws were tracked down to the Pine Springs Stage Station and besieged. During the gunfight, all four outlaws were killed. The gold was not found in the stage station, so the posse thought it was buried nearby. A search was made of the area, but no gold was said to have been found.

Rogers Lake Loot

The loot from two robberies was reportedly stashed on the southwest area of Rogers Lake near Flagstaff. The loot consisted of eight gold bars (each three inches by four inches by four inches), gold coins in a keg and a keg of silver coins.

Hostile Indians often attacked wagon trains. Some lost treasure was associated with these attacks. *Library of Congress.*

Roy Gardner's Treasure

Roy Gardner supposedly robbed a train and hid the loot near Flagstaff.

Sycamore Canyon/San Ignacio Mine/Geronimo's Lost Mine

See Yavapai County.

Wagon Train Valuables

In 1878, Indians attacked an eight-wagon train and killed all but two. The two survivors reportedly claimed that before the attack, the migrants had cached their valuables. The survivors did not know where the cache was. The treasure cache was said to have been hidden at Chavez Pass about twenty miles from the current town of Winslow. Treasure hunters searched the area over the years without reporting any treasure finds.

Gila County

Cibicue Apaches Lost Mine
Supposedly in southern Gila County.

Hensley's Loot
Outlaw Charles Hensley may have hidden $2,000 in loot (or possibly gold dust) near Mammoth Creek not far from Globe.

Lost Apache Mine
Said to be in the Tonto Basin on the north side of Mount Ord.

Lost Coyotero Mine
A legend claimed that this mine was in the northern part of the Tonto Basin near the Mogollon River.

Lost Felix Aubrey Gold Mine
Trader Felix (or Francis) Xavier Aubrey had many exploits in the Great Southwest. During one expedition, he and his party encountered a small group of Apaches in the Tonto Basin near the Mogollon Rim. The Apaches traded $1,500 worth of gold for a few pieces of old clothes. Upon questioning them about the source of the gold nuggets, the Apaches claimed that they picked up the nuggets near the Mogollon Rim.

Lost Golden Bullets Mine
Apaches reportedly made gold bullets from a gold deposit in the Tonto Basin below Promontory Butte near East Tonto Creek.

Lost Sanders Mine
This could be in the Sierra Ancha Mountains on the north side, about ten miles from the head of Coon Creek. See Lost Soldier Mine, following, as it's likely the same tale.

Lost Soldier Mine
In 1872, a U.S. Army detail camped on Diamond Creek (or North Fork of the Salt River), possibly on the north side of Mount Ord. One soldier called Sanders was sent to scout for raiding Apaches with stolen cattle. He followed their trail down the Salt River to the Sierra Ancha Mountains. He lost their trail and headed for Fort Apache. While going down Coon

Creek, he hit a dead end at a waterfall. Going up the canyon wall with his horse, he stumbled on a weathered quartz ledge containing gold. The ledge was eight inches wide and three yards deep. Sanders got some ore samples and returned to Fort Apache.

When Sanders finished his enlistment two years later, he went to Phoenix and had the ore samples assayed. They were very rich in gold. He left Phoenix with three partners to mine the gold ledge. Two of Sanders's partners parted company at old Camp Reno when a group of soldiers there warned them about a hostile Indian uprising. The two partners returned to Phoenix. Sanders and the other partner headed for his mine and were never heard from again. In the 1900s, some cowboys found two skeletons and a burned-down cabin. At the site, they found an ore sample with one inch of gold and the name Sanders carved on the ore sample. The cowboys later heard the story of Sanders and his lost mine, but they were unable to retrace their steps to the cabin.

Lost Tonto Trail Mine

Said to be in northwestern Gila County.

Miner's Lost Mine

In about 1871, a prospector called Miner found a placer gold deposit he claimed yielded seventeen ounces of gold from one shovelful of dirt and rock. He reported that it was near a butte that looked like a hat. Some believed this was Sombrero Butte. He led several prospecting companies but never found the lost placer deposit. One company searched up the San Pablo to the mouth of the San Carlos, up the San Carlos to its headwaters and then over to the Salt River. The search parties also went into the Tonto Basin to the mouth of Cherry Creek and along the Sierra Anchas. They found a hat-like butte but no placer gold.

Pedro Encinas Lost Mine

See Navajo County.

Graham County

Bonita's Treasure

The bandit Bonita supposedly stashed nineteen jack loads of gold and silver worth $22 million at the Meadows of Gold. This cache was reportedly about thirty miles southwest of Stafford near Bonita on the southwestern slopes of Mount Graham.

Bronco Bill Walters Cache

Outlaw William "Bronco Bill" Walters was a train robber who was shot and captured in July 1898 after an unsuccessful robbery in Grants, New Mexico. He was convicted and imprisoned until 1917. He worked as a cowboy until his death on June 16, 1921. He was said to have cached loot near Solomonville near his Arizona hideout before he was captured. It is likely that he recovered this cache after he got out of prison, but maybe not.

Clark Levering Treasure

Clark Levering reportedly cached hundreds of pounds of gold ore near where Fort Goodwin was located. Fort Goodwin was established in 1864 by Union California soldiers during the Civil War. It was near the Gila River and the community of Geronimo and Bylass. In 1954, one of these caches was said to have been uncovered.

Lost Adams Diggings

One of the most famous Old West lost mines was the Lost Adams Diggings. In August 1864, Adams was driving a wagon carrying freight between Los Angeles, California, and Tucson, Arizona Territory. His camp was raided by Indians west of Tucson. Adams killed one of the attacking Indians, but the Indians destroyed his wagon and freight. Adams managed to round up his horses and took them to a nearby Pima village. There Adams encountered twenty Californians who were talking to a Mexican with a deformed ear called Gotch Ear. Chiricahua Apaches raiding Sonora had captured Gotch Ear when he was young along with his brother. Gotch Ear was raised as an Apache but left the tribe when an Apache killed his brother. He reportedly told the Americans about an area rich in gold. He claimed that there was much more gold in that area than the California miners were recovering by panning nearby.

Gotch Ear negotiated with the California miners before disclosing the gold deposit's location. For a saddle horse, $100 in gold coins, a rifle, a pistol and two pack animals, Gotch Ear prepared to guide them to the secret site. Adams heard Gotch Ear's story and asked to go with them. Since Adams had horses, the Californians were happy to have Adams along. The miners traveled from the Mount Ord area. They crossed a wagon road that led to Fort Wingate. Fort Wingate had been established in 1860 as Fort Fauntleroy but later became known as Fort Lyon and then Fort Wingate. The miners encountered a narrow entrance into a zigzag canyon that could be hidden by a giant boulder. The riders could touch both sides of the narrow canyon at the same time. They camped for the night in the canyon. The next day, the miners reached a stream in the canyon containing a rich placer deposit and began mining. Gotch Ear was paid what he asked and left.

Adams and the Californians discovered that Apache Chief Nana, thirty warriors and their families were also in the zigzag canyon, which the Apaches called Sno-ta-hay. Chief Nana warned Adams and the miners that none of them were to go above a waterfall in the canyon. Later, the miners discovered that the horse and weapons they had given to Gotch Ear were in possession of Chief Nana's Apache warriors. The Apaches had murdered Gotch Ear. One miner later chased a stray horse above the waterfall and discovered an egg-shaped gold nugget there.

The miners constructed a cabin and cached their mined gold. Finally, their supplies were getting low, but there was still much gold to recover. John Brewer led a supply party of seven men to buy supplies at Fort Wingate. A German miner called Schaffer (or Schaeffer) accompanied the supply party with his share of the gold. Schaffer went to Fort Wingate with the supply party, left the party and traveled to Yuma, where he sold sixty-three pounds of gold. Schaffer returned to his home in Heidelberg, Germany.

When the supply party failed to return to the mining camp by the planned time, Adams and Bill Davidson left the diggings to determine what had happened to them. One story claimed that the man who was with Adams was named Landreau, not Bill Davidson. Adams and Davidson discovered that five of the supply party had been ambushed and killed by Apaches at the "closed door" entrance to the canyon.

As they headed back to the cabin farther up the canyon, Adams and Davidson heard screaming and Apaches yelling in the distance. Adams and Davidson crept up to a vantage point and looked down on several hundred Apaches attacking their comrades at the cabin, which had been set on fire by the Apaches. Outnumbered and not able to help, Adams and Davidson fled and escaped at night through the canyon "closed door" entrance.

Right: Chief Nana led hostile Apaches at the 1864 Lost Adams Diggings massacre. This photo was taken of him in 1886. *National Archives.*

Below: Fort Apache was instrumental in winning the wars against hostile Apaches. Photo from 1873. *Library of Congress.*

Adams had a large gold nugget with him when he fled the area. The Apaches were unable to track Adams and Davidson, as a sandstorm struck and hid their tracks. Adams and Davidson got lost while avoiding several bands of Apaches searching for them. After twelve to fourteen days of wandering, Adams and Davidson came across friendly people about twenty-six miles northwest of present Silver City, New Mexico. They were taken to a U.S. Army camp in the White Mountains, which later became Fort Apache. Fort Apache was not established until 1870. The military post that became known as Fort Apache was first called Camp Ord, then Camp Mogollon, then Camp Thomas and finally Fort Apache.

Adams saw five Apaches at Fort Apache. Enraged at having lived through the Apache attack, Adams killed three of them. Soldiers in the fort arrested Adams and placed him in the guardhouse to await trial a few days later. He escaped from the guardhouse on a stolen army horse. Adams went to Los Angeles.

Davidson meanwhile had traveled to Fort Whipple, where he told soldiers about the rich placer mine. Davidson hunted for his partner Adams and learned that he had gone to Los Angeles. Davidson reportedly died without ever returning to the diggings.

In 1874, Adams reportedly came back to look for what became known as the Lost Adams Diggings. With his new partner, Captain C.A. Shaw of Los Angeles, Adams, however, was unable to retrace the trail to the canyon since he had not paid attention to the route going in or coming out of the canyon. Ten years had passed. All that trauma clouded his memory. Captain Shaw checked out Adams's story by talking to an officer at Fort Wingate who remembered the party of miners that had come to Fort Wingate for supplies in 1864. Shaw heard that Adams had killed friendly Apaches at Fort Apache and had stolen a lieutenant's horse in order to escape. Adams later saw Chief Nana and some of the Apaches who had killed his partners. The Apaches refused to talk to Adams. Adams fled from the fort after he talked to Shaw, who told Adams that the U.S. Army still remembered he had murdered three friendly Apaches and had stolen an army horse.

John Brewer, who had been with the miners' supply party, had escaped the massacre by climbing up the canyon wall and reaching friendly Pueblo Indians. The Pueblos led Brewer to a village just south of Albuquerque, New Mexico, possibly Belen or Los Lunas. Brewer recovered his health and went to Colorado, where he married an Indian woman and raised a family.

Another variation of the Lost Adams Diggings story claimed that Adams's name was "Buck" Adams and that he had six companions, including Hein Hoffman, Dutch Brandel and Steve O'Connor. Five of these miners went to Fort Apache for supplies, and four of them were killed by Apaches on their way back to the diggings. Hoffman (who was called Schafer in the primary tale) left with his share of the gold before the party was attacked. Hoffman reportedly sold his gold for $12,000 and returned to Europe. Adams and Dutch (rather than Davidson) escaped the Apaches and encountered a party from Fort West who saved them. Dutch was supposedly later killed in a stampede.

The dates of the forts in the story are consistent with it taking place in 1864. J. Frank Dobie's book *Apache Gold and Yaqui Silver* devotes a lot of pages to the Lost Adams Diggings tale. Dobie extensively researched this story and gathered information from more than fifty people, as well as other sources.

A number of people claimed to have found the Lost Adams Diggings. Cowboy Jack Townsend reported that he found the Lost Adams Mine in New Mexico in 1894 while working out of Magdalena, New Mexico. W.C. Jameson's *The Canyon of Gold: Discovery of the Legendary Lost Adams Diggings* made a convincing case that Jim Peterson found the site with Chesser Creek and Chesser Gulch being the zigzag canyon the Apaches had called Sno-ta-hay. Chesser Creek is in the Apache-Sitgreaves National Forest and just east of US 191 and north of Clifton. Jameson visited the site with Peterson. It had a dilapidated shack built over a burned-out cabin, a stone chimney with two secret compartments to hide gold, a waterfall, meadows and a small amount of placer gold left. It fit most of the Lost Adams Diggings story, except for the entrance that could be blocked off. The creek had been mined out over the years.

The 1969 motion picture *Mackenna's Gold* was based around the Lost Adams Diggings story. Many have looked for this lost mine. Some believe that it was in Catron County, Cibola County or McKinley County, New Mexico, rather than in Arizona. Others thought it was in Apache County.

LOST BLACK BURRO MINE

See Navajo County.

MOUNTAIN OF APACHE SILVER

Mexican Pedro Encines was an Apache captive who claimed to have seen Apaches collecting silver in the Gila Mountains. It may have been near Gila Peak north of Fort Thomas. Encines escaped from the Apaches and returned to Mexico. He led a group of prospectors to look for the mountain of silver.

It was on the San Carlos Indian Reservation, which was not open for mining. The prospectors took an oath not to disclose the deposit's location until they got permission to mine the silver. Eventually, all the prospectors died without ever being able to mine the silver.

Wagon Train Cache
See Cochise County.

Greenlee County

Lost Black Burro Mine
See Navajo County.

Lost Chief Al-che-sa's Mine
Chief Al-che-sa of the Cibecue Apache tribe was said to have guarded a placer gold deposit on the San Carlos Reservation. He traded gold for goods he and his people needed. Chief Al-che-sa served as a U.S. Army scout for a while and helped get Geronimo and his band to surrender in 1886. Others believe that the source of his gold was the Lost Adams Diggings. See Lost Adams Diggings, Graham County.

Apache scouts at Fort Wingate who helped subdue hostile Indians. *National Archives.*

Lost Treasure of the Padres
See Coconino County.

Pedro Encinas Lost Mine
See Navajo County.

La Paz County

Frenchman's Lost Mine
See Yuma County.

Lost Glory Hole Mine
Said to be near Sulome.

Lost Pancho Mine
See Yuma County.

Lost Quartzsite Mine
Rumored to be near Quartzsite. See Yuma County.

Lost Sixshooter Mine No. 1
There are two Lost Sixshooter Mine stories in La Plaz County. One was a gold ore mine said to be located between Quartzsite and the Planet Mine. The Planet Mine was a copper mine discovered in 1863. The Planet Mine owner or superintendent was returning from dropping off investors at the Quartzsite stage station when a savage sandstorm hit. He lost his way. After wandering in no visibility, he took shelter behind a rock formation that had rich gold in quartz. He took a few samples, wrote descriptions of the area and left his two six-shooters at the rock formation to mark his claim on the ledge. He got back on his horse but fell off it at some point. His horse found its way back to the Planet Mine.

A search party from the mine found his body near Bouse. The gold samples in his pack assayed $25,000 per ton. The Lost Sixshooter Mine was said to be near the Bill Williams River between the Planet Mine and Quartzsite about fifteen miles northeast of Parker. Another version of this story has it in Yuma County.

This miner's monument marked his mining claim. *Library of Congress.*

Lost Sixshooter Mine No. 2

A second Lost Sixshooter Mine was a silver deposit between Ehrenburg and Wickenburg. Miner Billy Orne (or Orme) was in Ehrenberg with some Mexicans whom he and his partner Jacob Hamblin (or Hamlin) employed at their mine. Orne sent the employees to transport the supplies back to his mine while he went on a drunken spree. Eventually, Orne left Ehrenberg for the mine, but he was not completely sober and took along a canteen full of liquor to see him through his return trip.

On the first or second day of his trip out of Ehrenberg, he was still fuzzy-headed when he and his horse traveled up a flat wash and encountered a tall black reef he couldn't get over. He decided to bed down there to finish his liquor with his horse's reins tied around his waist. After falling asleep, his horse woke him up by pulling on the reins. Orne was angry and grabbed a nearby rock off the ground to throw at his horse. It was heavier than normal rocks its size, so he examined it closely. It was high-grade silver float that must have washed down from the reef above him.

He sobered up and put some of the ore in his pockets and saddlebags. He decided that he needed to stake a claim there, so he built a small pile of rocks. Not having paper for a mining claim, he put his six-shooter with his name carved on the gun handle inside the rock monument.

Billy Orne rode around the reef and found a corral with a water tank being refilled by a windmill. He could see a light in the distance, which was a lantern on a pole at Culling's Stage Station. His mind was still fuzzy and hung over as he reached the stage station.

When he was back at his mine, he told his story to his partner Hamblin. The two spent much time looking for the lost mine. Hamblin gave up the search, but Orne spent the rest of his life looking for the Lost Sixshooter Mine.

Lost Squaw Mine

An Indian "squaw" reportedly found a gold deposit between Wickenburg and Yuma. Ed Schiefflin, who discovered silver deposits at Tombstone, tried to get her to tell him where the gold deposit was located. She refused. Later, some Mexican prospectors threatened her and her family if she would not tell them where the gold deposit was. She led them to the northern Harquahala Mountains and refused to go farther. The prospectors beat her and killed several of her tribe members who tried to intervene. She escaped and disappeared.

The town of Ehrenberg on the Colorado River was where miners and prospectors got supplies. *New York Public Library.*

Later, a rich gold find was made in that area by others. Ed Schiefflin thought that this discovery was the site of the Lost Squaw Mine. This lost mine may be between Phoenix and Yuma. It's also said to be near the Harquahala Mountains.

Lost Wagon Gold Mine

Supposedly near Parker.

Sunlit Cave Treasure

Between Yuma and Ehrenberg, but closer to Ehrenberg (or twenty miles south of Ehrenberg), a legend claimed that the Sunlit Cave contained cached Spanish gold. The Sunlit Cave had an opening on a cliff face on the Arizona side of the Colorado River. In the midafternoon sun, the cave opening was visible when the sun was at a certain angle.

The Spanish mission and pueblo of La Purísima Concepción was established in 1780 on the California side of the Colorado River. A second Spanish pueblo and mission was nearby in California and was called San Pedro y San Pablo de Bicuner. During the July 1781 Yuma uprising, gold was rumored to have been hidden inside the Sunlit Cave in the form of raw gold nuggets, gold cast figures, vessels, crosses, chalices, crucifixes and holy images. This cache was from the looting of the Spanish towns and mines in the area. See Mission La Purísima Concepción and Mission Bicuner Treasures, Yuma County.

Maricopa County

Bronco Canyon Gold Nuggets

Two successful miners were rumored to have hidden about $75,000 in gold nuggets in 1891 close to a toadstool-like rock and a spring in the eastern part of Bronco Canyon. The miners reportedly were unable to locate their cache when they searched for it. Bronco Canyon is about thirty miles northwest of Fort McDowell.

Cal Madden's Lost Gold Vein

Prospector Cal Madden discovered a rich vein and brought samples of it to Wickenburg. The samples had free gold in quartz. Madden claimed that it was not too far from the Vulture Mine. Madden left town that night after getting supplies. After several weeks of not seeing or hearing from Madden, a search party was sent out from Wickenburg. They found Madden's mutilated and stripped body near Vulture Peak some twelve miles south of Wickenburg and six miles west of the Hassayampa River. It appeared that Indians had murdered him. People searched for his lost mine, but no one ever reported finding it.

About twenty years later, a Mexican prospector discovered a white gold–bearing vein that had been previously mined a few miles west of Vulture Creek. Samples from this vein did not match the ones Cal Madden had brought to town, so his gold vein may still be lost.

Gila Bend Spanish Mine

In the Maricopa Mountains area about fifteen miles east of Gila Bend, a legend claimed that the Spanish mined silver in the early 1700s. The mine was reportedly abandoned in about 1750.

Horse Thief Basin Treasure

This treasure was said to be in the Bradshaw Mountains.

Joaquin Compoy's Cave Treasure

A cavalry paymaster reportedly embezzled $26,000 in gold and hid it in the Estrella Mountains in a cave.

John Carroll's Lost Gold Mine

Fort McDowell trading post operator John Carroll traded with soldiers in the fort. One soldier used gold nuggets when he bought supplies. The soldier was such a good customer that John Carroll gave him credit until the soldier could return with more gold nuggets. Fort McDowell was set to close, and the soldier and his command were being transferred elsewhere. Carroll wanted the soldier to pay his bill. The soldier told Carroll that he couldn't leave the post to mine for more gold nuggets, but to bring his account up to date he would tell the trader where his placer mine was. John Carroll agreed to exchange the soldier's bill for the mine. They walked out onto the fort parade ground. The soldier pointed south to Weaver's Needle in the distance and told him to follow the line from their position south of Weaver's Needle—the first canyon on the other side of Weaver's Needle was where his mine was. The fort soon closed. John Carroll sold his business and went to look for the gold mine. He never found it. Some thought that the soldier gave him false directions to the mine. This is another lost mine said to be in the Superstition Mountains.

Knights of the Golden Circle Treasure

Warren Getler's and Bob Brewer's book *Rebel Gold* has several chapters devoted to the possibility of Knights of the Golden Circle hiding a Confederate treasure in the Superstition Mountains. They intertwine this with the tale of the Lost Dutchman Mine. See Lost Dutchman Mine.

The Lost Adams Diggings

See Graham County.

Lost Bear Hunters Mine

Supposedly in the Superstition Mountains.

Lost Black Maverick Mine

While chasing a black maverick cow in the late 1880s in the Four Peaks area northeast of Phoenix, cowboy Yaqui Valentino lassoed the maverick and found a rock infused with gold on the ground. He looked around and saw a shallow pit and the foundation rocks for an old cabin. He also found mining tools and the entrance to a mine. Back at the camp, he told his story. Some of the other cowboys wanted to know its location. Valentino refused to tell them and left the outfit. Later, he told his friend Henry Hardt about the mine and agreed to partner with him to mine the site. When they reached the Four Peaks area, Valentino refused to go further, as he had just dreamed that Apaches would kill him if he mined there. Valentino died a few months later.

Lost Dr. Thorne Mine

Young Dr. Abraham Thorne (or Dr. Thomas in another variation of this tale) was captured by a band of Tonto Apaches in 1861 (or 1865) so he could treat tribal members with white medicine when Indian medicine did not work. Dr. Thorne treated and saved many ill Apache women and children while their men were out raiding miners and settlers.

The grateful Apaches freed Dr. Thorne for curing their ill tribe members. Before being released, Dr. Thorne was blindfolded, and six warriors escorted him to their gold mine called Pesh-La-Chi. The mine may be near the Salt River, between the Superstition Mountains and the Mazatzal Mountains. The mine was located in a narrow canyon with an eighteen-inch gold-filled quartz vein running across the canyon. He estimated that the mine was about twenty miles from Fort McDowell. After the blindfold was taken off, Dr. Thorne was at the base of a canyon with a quartz vein that was about half gold. He recovered a sack full of gold there. He claimed he saw what could have been the tip of Weaver's Needle several miles to the south. Later, he said his blindfold slipped from his eyes. He saw Weaver's Needle and the ruins of a stone building next to the trail, where a small stream joined a larger one. Dr. Thorne later sold this gold for about $6,000 to the San Francisco Mint. This would have been about twenty pounds of gold.

After the hostile Apaches stopped their raids and were rounded up, in about 1883, Dr. Thorne returned to the area with a prospecting group, but he never could retrace his steps to the gold deposit. He also reportedly claimed that the mine was on the west or south side of the Four Peaks. Dr. Thorne never found his lost mine.

Another version of this tale claimed that in 1865, Dr. Abraham Thorne worked at Fort McDowell as a civilian physician taking care of Apaches. See Lost Dutchman Mine and Lost Peralta Mine.

Lost Dutchman Mine

The famous prospector associated with the Lost Dutchman Mine was a German known as Jacob (or Jakob) Waltz (or von Walzer, Walz or Walls) who became known as the Old Dutchman ("Deutschman," or German mispronounced by Americans). He was born in 1810 and grew up near Stuttgart, Germany. The Old Dutchman was said to have been a mining engineer trained at Heidelberg and had mined in Prussia and Australia before ending up in America about 1845 at New York City. He went west during the California Gold Rush. He was said to have also worked at gold fields in North Carolina and Georgia, lived in Natchez, Mississippi, and prospected for gold in California's Sierra Nevadas. He also prospected in the Los Angeles area in the San Gabriel Mountains. He was said to have fought for the Confederacy during the Civil War.

Waltz moved to Arizona Territory in 1863. One version says that German immigrants Jacob Waltz and Jacob Weiser (or Werser or Wisner) were Confederate veterans who helped save Don Miguel Peralta in a fight. Waltz was said to have filed mining claims in 1863 and 1865 near Prescott, which do not appear to have been rich deposits.

In about 1871, Waltz had an Apache wife named Ken-tee. Waltz had worked at the rich Vulture Gold Mine at Wickenburg. He was fired for smuggling gold from the Vulture Mine. A number of miners were involved in the high grading crime, and about $175,000 worth of gold ore was recovered. Some think that his lost mine story was a cover for his illegal high grading.

Waltz and Ken-tee went up into the mountains and returned with several burro loads of gold from a hidden mine after several weeks. The gold was sent to San Francisco. Some miners and settlers thought that the Old Dutchman had found the Lost Peralta Mine. Apaches raided Waltz's home and took Ken-tee with them for disclosing the location of the gold deposit, which may have been the Peralta mine. Waltz and a party recovered her from the Apache war party, but the Apaches were said to have cut out her tongue. She died in Waltz's arms.

Waltz then moved to a location a few miles from the Superstition Mountains. He homesteaded 160 acres on the north side of the Salt River near Phoenix. The Old Dutchman became a hermit and a drunk in Phoenix. He had a reputation as a brawler in the bars, and his fame spread about his mine up in the Superstition Mountains. About three years after Ken-tee's murder, Jacob Weiser joined Waltz in Phoenix. Weiser and Waltz agreed to share any recovered gold from the Peralta mine with Don Miguel Peralta, who gave them a map to the site. See Lost Peralta Mine.

According to one story, Waltz and Weiser easily found the mine, but two dark-skinned men were digging at the site in 1879. Thinking that the two men were Apaches, Waltz and Weiser reportedly shot and killed them. The two dead men were actually Peralta employees who were freelancing (high grading) some gold from the Peralta gold mine. Waltz and Weiser returned to Phoenix within a month with gold concentrate in sacks, which they sent by Wells Fargo to the San Francisco Mint. Weiser and Waltz reportedly recovered $60,000 in gold and shared half of it with Don Miguel Peralta.

They made another successful trip and returned to Phoenix with more gold. Apache Indians attacked Waltz and Weiser in their camp one night. Weiser got an arrow through his left arm and chest. Weiser made it to Dr. John D. Walker's home with the help of friendly Pima Indians. Weiser thought that Waltz had been killed by Apaches and reportedly gave Dr. Walker a map to the mine. Weiser died the next morning. Another version of the story said that he died several months later of complications. Sometime later, Dr. Walker showed the map to a newspaperman, Thomas F. Weed, who made a copy of the map and later told Sims Ely about the tale. Ely and his friend Jim Bark looked for the Lost Dutchman mine over the next twenty-five years, but without a copy of the map.

Waltz had escaped the attack unharmed in his shirt, shoes and stockings, but another version of the tale said that Waltz was not in camp when the Indians attacked, but rather was getting supplies from a nearby town. Waltz reportedly returned to their camp and removed one of the three gold caches he and his partner had hidden.

When Waltz went to the mountains to recover more gold, he was often followed. He had a chicken ranch near Phoenix. There were rumors that he may have killed some of those who followed him. Waltz was said to have received $254,000 from the U.S. Mint between 1879 and 1885. Some researchers have not been able to find any evidence of this.

One prospector called Joe Deering claimed that he found a hole in the mountain that was Waltz's mine, but Deering died in an accident. Two young men said to have been ex-soldiers brought gold in saddlebags to Pinal in the summer of 1880. The two men had planned to travel by foot over the Superstition Mountains to Florence to apply for work at the Silver King Mine. En route they said they found a funnel-shaped opening in the mountains with a rich gold vein and had gathered as much gold as they could. The mine was north of a rock pinnacle that could have been Weaver's Needle. They left after getting supplies and were found ten days later, naked and dead. Although it looked as if Apaches had killed them, some suspected that they were murdered by Waltz to protect his mine. Others noticed that a local trader suddenly had riches, and they suspected him. This is called the Lost Two Soldiers Mine by some, but sounds like it was one of the Peralta mines. See Lost Two Soldiers Mine.

Some who knew Jacob Waltz said that there was never any Lost Dutchman Mine and that he lived in poverty in an adobe house near the intersection of present Sixteenth Street and Henshaw Road in Phoenix late in his life. His adobe house was actually a hut with rustic furnishings.

Waltz was said to have recovered $15,000 in gold from a cache in 1890. In the Salt River flood of February 1891, Waltz's adobe was destroyed. He had to climb a tree and hold on for dear life for several days before he was rescued. Waltz became sick with pneumonia and died on October 25, 1891, at the home of a woman, Mrs. Charles Thomas, who was called Helena Thomas (also called Julia Holmes or Julia Thomas Schaeffer in some versions). Helena Thomas took care of Waltz. He left her $15,000 and gave directions to his mine to some of his friends. Another version of the story from Ely was that Waltz gave her $1,400 in gold, which he recovered from its burial site at his home.

There was a story that Waltz took a liking to a young man from back east who was out west trying to recover from tuberculosis. The young man then returned back east. Several women appeared in the Phoenix area years later and were thought to be sisters of Waltz's friend. They had a map of a mining claim that came from Waltz, but nothing appears to have resulted from their trip concerning the Lost Dutchman Mine. Dick Holmes said on his deathbed that Waltz confessed to murdering his nephew Julius, who had come over from Germany, as the young man talked too much.

Directions were passed down to countless people who have searched for the Lost Dutchman Mine are: "The mine is near the hideout cave. One mile from the cave, there is a rock with a natural face looking east. To the South is Weaver's Needle. Follow the right of the canyons but not far. The mine faces west." The land around the mine was said to be extremely rough—it would be easy to miss the mine.

Further descriptions include the following: "The mine can be found at the spot on which the shadow of the tip of Weaver's Needle falls on many places at four o'clock." Many people have looked for much of their life without finding the mine.

The entrance to the mine was said to be like a funnel, with the broad end at the top. Shelves were cut along the walls to help load the burros with gold. A tunnel ran from the mountainside to the bottom of the shaft. The mine had a 1.5-foot-wide rose quartz vein, which held the gold.

At the site of the Peralta massacre, there was a huge boulder, and Weiser was said to have told a grocer that the mine shaft was just a little west of this massacre site. Charles Hall of Denver became interested in the site, paid $50,000 for mining claims in the area and opened what was known as the Goldfield Mine. The Goldfield Mine recovered more than $3 million in gold over a few years using mining equipment. Some believe that this may have been the Lost Dutchman Mine.

Sims Ely and Jim Bark uncovered many stories about the Lost Dutchman Mine and spent much of their time looking for it in the Superstition Mountains. Jim Bark bought a large ranch in 1890 in the Superstition Mountains and visited Helena Thomas's bakery in Phoenix on business trips, where he undoubtedly got information on the old Dutchman. Sims Ely wrote a book, *The Lost Dutchman Mine*, which detailed his research and search over several decades.

Another searcher, Adolph Ruth, a civil servant from Washington, D.C., went to the Superstition Mountains in 1931 with an old map that was said to have come from the Peralta family. Ruth's skull, with two bullet holes in it, was found in December 1931 in West Boulder Canyon six months after he had been dropped off in the mountains. His body and belongings were discovered one month later some distance from where his skull was found. A little notebook was found that had Weaver's Needle as the center of the search with a five-mile radius. The notebook had the following: "The first gorge on the south side from the west end of the range—they found a blazed trail which led them northward over a high ridge, then downward into a long canyon running North and finally to a tributary canyon very deep, rocky and densely covered with a continuous thicket of scrub oak…about two hundred feet across from a cave." At the bottom of the page, he wrote, in Latin, Julius Caesar's famous words: "Veni, vidi, vici" (I came, I saw, I conquered).

In 1940, a group of prospectors was said to have found nuggets cemented in gravel in the Superstition Mountains and worked out the deposit. After World War II, Alfred Strong Lewis, a mining engineer, explored the Goldfield Mine area, and at the base of a large boulder, he noticed something odd. He dynamited the boulder and found an old mining shaft under the boulder. He was near the Goldfield Mine and about one mile from the Peralta massacre ground. The mineshaft was timbered with ironwood that had been cut by axe. At seventy-five feet, he found a rich gold lode. He knew that he had found Peralta's lost mine. He reportedly recovered $42,000 in gold and then broke into a larger, modern shaft, which he thought was Hall's shaft, as the rest of the area had already been mined. The site was said to be now under Goldfield Lake.

In June 1947, James A. Crarey, a sixty-two-year-old retired photographer from Phoenix, was dropped off by helicopter to spend a few days looking for the Lost Dutchman Mine. Crarey disappeared, and two prospectors found his skeleton in February 1948. The skull was later found some distance from the main skeleton.

In 1949, a hiker found several cryptic tablets with markings on them that some thought was Spanish in origin. Others thought that they might have been clues to a Knights of the Golden Circle treasure. The tablets were featured in a 1964 *Life* magazine article. The tablets are now in the Arizona Mining and Mineral Museum at Phoenix. The article said that they were found in 1956 by a vacationing Oregon policeman. A businessman with the false name of Travis Marlowe acquired three tablets and continued the search.

Some think that Waltz was an agent of the Knights of the Golden Circle who was guarding several treasure caches that the Knights of the Golden Circle had hidden in and around Arizona's Superstition Mountains. These treasures were said to have a number of markers set up in the mountains and desert as clues to their location.

In 1959, treasure hunter Benjamin Ferreira murdered his partner, Stanley Fernandez, while they looked for the Lost Dutchman Mine. Some believe that the large number of deaths of treasure hunters looking for the Lost Dutchman may have been due in part to sentinels that guarded the treasure.

Many expeditions have looked for lost mines and treasures in the Superstition Mountains without success. Some have found evidence of mines and gold in the area. Most of the area is now part of the Superstition Wilderness and Tonto National Forest. Many books and articles have been written about the Lost Dutchman Mine. One book says that the mine was actually found and was the Bull Dog Mine near Goldfield. Another book claimed that the mine is northeast of Carefree. Other possible locations are the Gloriana Mine or Valenciana Mine, just west of Interstate 17. See Lost Dr. Thorne Mine, the Lost Peralta Mine, the Lost Two Soldiers Mine, Lost Wagoner Mine and Knights of the Golden Circle Treasure. Whether this lost mine has been found or still remains to be found, the Lost Dutchman Mine remains the greatest lost mine tale in the United States, if not the world.

LOST EPILEPTIC GOLD MINE AND TREASURE

A cache of $50,000 in gold bars was rumored to be hidden in or near this lost mine in the Estrella Mountains.

LOST GONZALES MINE

Supposed to be near Sombrero Peak in the Superstition Mountains.

LOST JACK SWILLING MINE

Jack Swilling's mine was said to be worth $1,000 per ton of gold quartz in 1874 in the Vulture Peak region between Phoenix and Wickenburg.

LOST JENKINS MINE

Reportedly in the Superstition Mountains.

LOST LORD DUPPA MINE

Supposedly near Wickenburg. This could be in Yavapai County.

LOST MAD SQUAW GOLD MINE

May be in the Gila Bend Mountains.

LOST MANJE MINE

A legend put the location near Mobile.

Lost Mine of Hat Mountain

Rumored to be in southern Maricopa County.

Lost Miner Gold Mine

This mine was said to have been in the Superstition Mountains.

Lost Peralta Mine

Don Pedro Peralta de Cordoba was very wealthy and owned a number of very rich mines in Sonora. Pedro Peralta became the governor of Santa Fe in 1608. The Peralta family had Spanish land grants. In 1748, Spanish King Ferdinand VI granted about 3,750 square miles of land to the first Don Miguel Peralta due to his loyal service to the Spanish Crown. In 1776, Don Miguel Peralta became the Baron de Colorado. When the Baron de Colorado died in 1788, his lands were inherited by his son. According to some, Don Enrico Peralta mined what later became known as the Lost Dutchman Mine. Don Enrico Peralta's son was Don Miguel Peralta. There are many variations of the Peralta family stories with the Lost Dutchman Mine with different Peralta family members. A few Peraltas have the same first name over several different generations, which causes confusion about when events happened and which Peralta was involved in which event.

In 1845 or 1846, Don Miguel Peralta and Pedro Peralta, descendants of Don Pedro Peralta, reportedly discovered gold in the Superstition Mountains northeast of present Apache Junction. One site was at the junction of a stream (possibly La Barge Creek) and Rio Salado, near Mormon Flat. Pedro Peralta was said to have followed gold float upstream, up La Barge Canyon to Boulder Creek and then up Needle Creek, below Weaver's Needle. One to two miles to the north was a hat-shaped peak called La Sombrera.

Pedro Peralta reportedly found a gold deposit on the east slope of a black-topped mountain about 1.5 miles north of La Sombrera where there were two large outcrops of red gold quartz. A second gold deposit was reportedly on the north side, with a third on the southwestern slope.

They called the new mine Sombrera after the shape of a nearby mountain peak, near Weaver's Needle, which is a 4,553-foot-high pinnacle. Mexican miners came to the area to dig for gold, much to the displeasure of the Apaches. A mining camp with a smelter was said to have been established on the Salt River, near the mine. It was said that Don Peralta had as many as eighteen different mines within his vast land grant.

During the Mexican-American War, U.S. troops under General Doniphan and General Kearney invaded and occupied the area in 1846. After the war, a battered Mexico ceded most of Arizona to the United States under the Treaty of Guadalupe Hidalgo. The vast Peralta land grant became part of the United States.

Large quantities of gold were reportedly recovered from several Peralta mines, but the Apaches decided that they had enough from the Mexican miners. Miguel Peralta heard rumors of a proposed Apache attack and decided to withdraw from the area for a while. In September 1848, Indians attacked arrastras associated with the Peralta mines. Miguel Peralta was said to have buried gold near one mine and marked the site on a map and then hid the mine entrance. Ramon and Manuel Peralta left their brother Pedro to return home. Miguel Peralta may have had sixty-eight men and two hundred mules in the Superstition Mountains at the mine.

Peralta and his men withdrew to a more easily defended camp up in the mountains. A pack train to carry out gold and men was assembled. Mangas Coloradas, leader of the Chiricahua Apaches, and Apache Chief Cochise ambushed Peralta and his men as they sought to escape. The battle took place at the base of high cliffs. Miguel Peralta and all his men were killed. The gold on the back of the burros was scattered all over the area. Burros were killed or captured, buckskin bags from the animals were taken and their gold was left behind on the ground.

Manuel Peralta, on his deathbed in Sonora, Mexico, told his son Ramon Peralta y Gonzales, who was living in Maricopa, Arizona, about the Peralta family's lost mines. Manuel gave his son a treasure map of his family's lost Arizona mine. Ramon needed money to prospect for and mine the gold, so he contacted Charles M. Clark, Maricopa's telegraph operator, who got a look at the map. According to Clark, the map was a sketch the Four Peaks on the north, with Weaver's Needle on the south. A line between the two markers intersected the Salt River about midway, where the name Fresno was marked on a tributary canyon. Four crosses were around the junction of the tributary, along with the word *mina*.

Manual Peralta did not find the lost mine, but he did find skeletons from the massacre of his family's miners and concentrated gold from the mine scattered about in rotting sacks. He put the concentrate on his pack animal and returned to civilization. He gave Clark a share of the gold and then moved to California to live off his share. Clark continually searched for the Lost Peralta Mine for years. He looked around La Barge Canyon, a tributary of Tortilla Creek, which could be the aforementioned Fresno Canyon. In 1930, Manual Peralta returned again to look for the lost mine but failed to find it.

Ramon Peralta gave these paraphrased directions to a few prospector friends:

> [F]*rom the desert they would have to go up the first deep canyon from the western end of the range, climb northward over the backbone of the western end of the range, climb northward over the backbone of the range itself until they came within sight of a huge sombrero-shaped peak dead ahead, travel downward past the base of the peak into a canyon* [East Boulder] *running northward until at last they found on the east side the entrance to a tributary canyon which was very deep, pot-holed and densely wooded with scrub oak. Then they were to turn about and go back southward up this tributary* [Needle] *canyon until they reached a point where the outlines of the hat-shaped peak to the south and the black-topped mountain to the west both matched from the same place the outlines upon the map. Near this spot they would find a marker upon the end of a rocky ledge. And the marker would be pointing to nearby mines!*

U.S. Army troops were said to have found some skeletons from the massacre in 1850. Two gold prospectors with the last name of Hurley and O'Connor found a burro skeleton with a pack of gold in the 1850s from the massacre in an area known as Goldfield. Searching the area, they found another burro skeleton and two more packs of gold. They refined the gold, took it to the U.S. Mint in San Francisco and received $37,000 for the gold. They returned to the site and found other packs of gold left by Peralta and his ill-fated miners. The last pack of gold was found in 1914 by C.H. Silverlocke and a partner. The mule load of gold in the lava beds was worth $18,000. It was also thought to be part of Peralta's gold that was dumped from his burros. See Lost Dutchman Mine and Lost Dr. Thornton Mine.

Lost Pick Mine

May be in Bronco Canyon about twenty-five miles northwest of Fort McDowell. See Bronco Canyon Lost Gold. This could be in Yavapai County.

Lost Silver Mine of the Stars

Legends indicate that it is in the Estrella Mountains.

Lost Squaw Hollow Gold Ledge

In 1864, Colonel King S. Woolsey, an aide to the Arizona Territory governor, led three expeditions against the Tonto, Yavapais and Pinalenos Apaches.

U.S. Army soldiers fought hostile Indians throughout Arizona. *Library of Congress.*

Woolsey had a ranch on the Agua Fria River near present Dewey. Woolsey arrived in Arizona Territory in 1860 and became a rich, influential politician. Woolsey was said to have had secessionist leanings during the Civil War. On one expedition, Woolsey and a small group of men including Judge J.T. Alsop fought an Apache band. Woolsey's group camped in Squaw Hollow, about forty miles north of Phoenix in the Camp Creek area, about ten miles south of Bronco Canyon, between the Agua Flint River and Verde River. Some men left their camp to prospect for gold. They returned to camp a few hours later with rich gold ore. Judge Alsop said that it was the richest gold ore he had ever seen.

Apaches suddenly attacked in force, and Colonel Woolsey's men fled. The "Official Records" report that on May 1, 1864, one of Woolsey's expeditions killed thirty-one Apaches. Woolsey led and participated with Union California troops on Indian raids in 1864 and 1865.

The Apaches were not subdued for many years and prevented those who knew about the gold ore from returning. Years later, Judge Alsop returned to the area and located his old camp on Camp Creek, but since he was not with the party that found the gold, he could not locate the gold ledge. Woolsey's reports of gold enticed prospectors to enter Apache-held lands.

A Mexican sheepherder later reportedly camped at Squaw Hollow one night and found that a man was living in a cabin. The man was working a rich mine nearby. The miner said he carried the ore to his cabin by burro, ground up the ore in an iron mortar and washed it with water from the creek. The Mexican sheepherder returned to the area many years later, but the prospector was gone and the cabin was in ruins with a small pile of tailings near it. The Squaw Hollow area is highly mineralized and has been extensively mined. It is possible that the Lost Squaw Hollow Gold Ledge has been mined. It could be in Yavapai County.

Lost Squaw Mine

See La Paz County.

Lost Three Dutchman Mine

Three Dutchmen reportedly traded stolen horses to Apache Indians for a gold mine in the Gila River country, where they secretly mined gold without permission of the Spanish government. Spanish Governor Diego de Peralta reportedly sent out soldiers who ambushed the three Dutchmen in 1621 between El Paso and Cananea. Two Dutchmen were killed. All their mined gold being transported was confiscated. The third Dutchman was mortally wounded. Before dying, he told a priest at a Socorro mission the story of the lost gold mine. It could be in Yuma County.

Lost Two Soldiers Mine

Several U.S. Army soldiers were said to have found a rich gold deposit and mined some gold from it. Indians attacked and killed them. When their bodies were found, so was the gold they had mined. They were not killed at the mine site, so its location has been a mystery. Some think that it was in La Barge Canyon in the Superstition Mountains. See Lost Dutchman Mine.

Lost Wagoner Mine

In 1894, a prospector called Wagoner was often picked up at a desolate location along the road by the Pinal-Mesa stagecoach on the west side of the Superstition Mountains. He carried two empty sacks, as he was going to replenish his supplies each time. One day, he changed his pickup location to a site near Whitlow's Ranch. Instead of empty sacks, Wagoner carried heavy suitcases. The stage driver named Mullins helped him load the suitcases onto the stagecoach, as Wagoner was ill and weak. Wagoner said that it was his last trip and let the driver see the suitcases' content. They carried rich gold ore. He told the driver general locations to his mine, which was a rose quartz outcrop hidden behind newly planted trees. The stage driver looked for the mine but never found it.

Before finding the mine, Wagoner was said to have camped in the center of La Barge Canyon some three miles east of Weaver's Needle and due north of Miner's Needle. Wagoner then traveled due east over broken hills, after about an hour's walk. The mine may be within a triangle formed by Weaver's Needle, Picacho Butte and Miner's Needle.

Twenty years later, a man showed up in the area with a map to the mine, which he got from Wagoner before he passed. The map showed the mine in La Barge Canyon, but the man never found the mine. Some believe that this might have been the Lost Dutchman Mine, as La Barge knew Jacob Waltz. The Old Dutchman and La Barge had a camp in La Barge Canyon. Supposedly, the mine is between Weaver's Needle and Miner's Needle on the south side of La Barge Canyon. It could be in Pinal County. See the Lost Dutchman Mine.

Marjorie Jackson Robbery Loot

Marjorie Viola O'Connel Jackson was the wife of rich businessman Chester Jackson, who had inherited his father's Standard Grocery store chain. Chester's father, Lafayette Andrew Jackson, was murdered in a 1931 robbery at one of his stores. Chester Jackson sold the grocery store chain in 1947. Chester Jackson died in 1970, leaving his wife very rich, as his estate was reportedly worth more than $25 million. His wife reportedly got about $14 million in cash.

After there was an embezzlement in her account at the bank, Marjorie Jackson withdrew about $8.6 million in cash over four months from the Indianapolis National Bank. In her house, she hid the money in her dresser, in trash cans, trash bags, toolboxes and vacuum cleaner bags. She put aluminum foil over vents and doorknobs in her house. She had a table set for Jesus Christ and a number of gifts wrapped for Jesus Christ.

In 1977, Howard R. (Billy Joe) Willard and Manuel Lee Robinson robbed Marjorie Jackson of $3 million to $6 million in cash and jewelry at her home in the 6400 block of Spring Hill Road in Indianapolis, Indiana. Two teenage boys had stolen $800,000 and jewelry from her home several months before she was robbed by Willard and Robinson. Willard was thirty-eight and was from Morresville. Willard and Robinson made several trips to her house during the robbery, which started on May 1, 1977. Willard shot Marjorie Jackson with a .22 rifle, and she bled to death. The two robbers set fire to her house, but the fire smoldered for days. When the fire department and police appeared, they found Marjorie Jackson's body along with much still hidden cash that the robbers had missed.

The robbers went on a buying spree and paid cash for multiple new cars. A suspicious salesman reported them to the police. Robinson had $1.6 million in cash in a suitcase in his apartment when the police interrogated him.

Robinson claimed that he was given the money by a man he didn't know. He eventually gave the police a phone number, which was the phone number of Willard's ex-wife, who was still having a relationship with Robinson's partner, Howard R. Willard. Robinson later claimed that the police stole $450,000 in cash from him.

The police tracked Willard and his ex-wife to Arizona, where they had bought two RVs for about $50,000 in cash. Willard's ex-wife cooperated with the FBI office out of Phoenix. She took them to a location off Interstate 17 north of Phoenix, where the police recovered $1.7 million in cash in two boxes. She said that Willard had talked to famous attorney F. Lee Bailey, who recommended they hide the money in several locations.

One writer's book claimed that a now dead FBI agent on the case likely stole some of the cash. This FBI agent allegedly deposited the money in a Swiss bank account and then transferred the money to the Netherland Antilles and bought real estate, the title for which was held by an offshore holding company. Part of the FBI files on this case were mysteriously destroyed.

Willard was convicted of murder in Indiana and got a life sentence. He died in prison in June 1987 while jogging. Robinson went to prison for burglary and arson. He was released in 1988 but returned to prison in 1990 for a ten-year sentence.

There seems to have been more than $1 million in cash that was never recovered. Some speculate that it was hidden in Arizona near where the FBI recovered the $1.7 million. This could be in Yavapai County.

Puncher Bob's Lost Gold Mine

This mine was supposedly near Four Peaks.

Valenzuela Gang Loot

The outlaw Valenzuela Gang reportedly hid $25,000 in gold in the Wittman area.

Mohave County

Fort Mohave Caches

Several caches of gold nuggets were supposedly hidden in the north part of Fort Mohave near the carpenter shop. The fort was burned in 1861 and

Needles Mountains and Colorado River, not far from Fort Mohave. *New York Public Library.*

rebuilt in 1863. When it was abandoned in 1861, Peter R. Brady buried books from the post library wrapped in a tarp, two barrels of whiskey and a few cases of wine under the commissary before burning the building. Fort Mohave was abandoned as a U.S. Army post in 1890. It is now the Needles Indian Reservation. It is hard to believe that the cache under the commissary building was never dug up.

HIDDEN CACHES

Caches from Mormon massacres and the Wild Bunch Gang were reportedly hidden near Littlefield. Some Mormon money was said to be hidden near the Virgin River.

LOST AND FOUND GOLD CACHES

A nail keg full of gold was discovered near Bullhead City, but a cache of gold nuggets and gold ore was said to also be cached on a hill a few miles southeast of Bullhead City.

LOST CONDUCTOR MINE

A legend indicated that this gold deposit was in yellow clay near the Colorado River south of Topock.

Lost Nazi Gold

During World War II, Nazi officers were supposedly in Sonora, Mexico, with millions of dollars ($300 million in gold bullion) to generate sympathy for Nazi Germany in Mexico. Some of this treasure was rumored to have been taken into the United States near Kingman, Arizona. When the war ended, the Nazis vanished, and so did their gold. This is a hard story to believe, but there may be some basis for it. See Yavapai County.

Lost Negro Mine

May be near Wikieup.

Lost Nugget Mine

Said to be near Wikieup or Topock.

Lost Stagecoach Bullion

In June 1880, a stagecoach left the Beale Spring Stage Station bound for Needles, California, with a cargo reportedly of $200,000 in gold bullion. Hualapai Joe Desredo and two other outlaws held up the stagecoach at night and took the gold. The stagecoach, the driver and its passenger supposedly vanished. Later, Desredo was mortally wounded in a gunfight and claimed that he was involved in stealing the gold from the stagecoach but did not hurt the driver and passenger. He said that after the robbery the stagecoach drove off into the night, but he heard strange sounds in distance like breaking wood and rocks making noise.

Desredo and his two accomplices in the robbery all died shortly after the robbery in shootouts with the law. What happened to the gold is unknown. Maurice Kildare wrote about this story after he heard it in 1940 from Max Bordon, who claimed to have found the washed up remains of what looked to have been a stagecoach along with human bones in a crevice in a steep wash near the robbery site. It appears that the driver got lost off the road and drove the stagecoach into the crevice.

Lost Two Brothers Mine

When World War II began, two brothers from Los Angeles were said to have found rich gold ore in the upper Cerbat Mountains north of Chloride. On a return trip, a woman went with them as they used explosives to break up ore. With two sacks of rich gold ore, they returned home after hiding the diggings. A friend assayed the ore and declared it to be rich ore. The two brothers were drafted into the U.S. Army. Both died in the Pacific during the war. Their friend, the assayer, talked the woman who had been to the site of their mine to help search for it. They searched for the mine but never reported finding it.

Lost Whitlesy Mine

Sam Whitlesy discovered a rich gold ledge and told others about it. It was claimed to have assayed $35,000 per ton in 1894. It was supposed to be in the Black Mountains, about two miles from 3,652-foot-high Sitgreaves Pass, not far from Oatman. Two men tailed Whitlesy hoping to find out the location of his rich mine. In a fight, Sam Whitlesy killed the two men but was mortally wounded and never gave directions to his mine before dying.

Montezuma's Treasure

One of the many Montezuma treasures was said to be hidden in cave near an Indian village on the south bank of the Colorado River, at the Lower Granite Gorge of the Grand Canyon, a few miles to three miles east of Pierce (or Pearce) Ferry. Spanish Governor Onate reportedly searched for Montezuma's treasure in 1604. In 1865, Jim White went down the Colorado River in a raft and supposedly came across this treasure in a cave. Montezuma's Aztec treasure consisted of thousands of gold statues and objects. Jim White left the cave and became lost. He was starving and delirious when he reached civilization. White was never able to find his way back to the site of Montezuma's treasure.

Smith's Cache

Cattleman Hiram Smith reportedly buried gold coins in a sand dune on the Colorado River. The location is now believed to be under Lake Mohave.

Navajo County

Carpenter's Lost Silver Mine

A story claimed that Mark Carpenter had a silver mine and cached silver ore along Silver Creek not far from Shumway. While en route to St. John with a burro packing silver ore and supplies, a band of Apaches attacked him. He was wounded, and the Apaches took his horse and supplies. He managed to get on his burro and was found by soldiers, but he died soon thereafter. People searched for the source of his silver ore but never reported finding it.

Lost Black Burro Mine

In 1862, three prospectors were on the Old Mansfield Trail, which runs from the San Francisco River in Catron County, New Mexico, to Eagle Creek in Graham County. This trail was used by prospectors and miners. The three supposedly discovered a lone black burro with a new-looking packsaddle grazing off the trail. The burro carried rich ore in two rawhide sacks. The men expected the owner to show up to reclaim his burro and ore, so they camped there for the night. When no one showed up by morning, they figured Apaches had killed him. They continued on their way and were attacked by Apaches, who killed two of the three men. The surviving prospector made it to a small settlement. Due to the Apache uprising, no one dared to look for the source of the gold at that time. This could be in Apache County or Greenlee County.

Lost Pea-Sized Gold Nuggets

A rich deposit of pea-sized gold nuggets was reportedly found in 1874, but Indian revolts prevented the finder from recovering all the nuggets. This was said to be near Winslow, upstream from Chevelon in a creek.

Lost Silver Monument Valley Mine/Lost Pish-La-Ki Mine

In 1880, prospectors Merrick and Mitchell were killed by a band of Navajos led by Chief Haskaninni (Angry One) in the Monument Valley. The two were said to have been former U.S. soldiers. The prospectors had looked for and reportedly found a silver deposit that the Navajos used to make silver ornaments. The other name for the mine was the Lost Pish-la-Ki Mine. The ore from this mine was said to have been black. It was reportedly located near Mitchell Butte. This could be in Apache County.

Pedro Encinas Lost Mine

This could be near Fort Apache or in Gila County or Greenlee County.

Turquoise Shrine Treasure

Said to be near Holbrook.

Wolf's Cache

German Herman Wolf owned a trading post northeast of Canyon Diablo on the Little Colorado River. His business was near the California–Santa Fe Trail. He died in about 1899 and was reportedly very wealthy after trading with Indians since 1869. Some believe that he hid $25,000 to $50,000 (or

$250,000) in coins in the area near his trading post. A few coins have been reportedly recovered in that area. Mexican silver coins and U.S. gold coins were found in 1901 and 1966 in buckets that may have been part of his caches.

Pima County

Arivaca Treasure

In the corner of an old Arivaca adobe house, padres reportedly hid gold and silver bullion before an Indian attack during Spanish colonial days. The Indians killed many in Arivaca. The padres fled south to Mexico City and never returned for their treasure. See Lost Sapori Mine/Treasure.

Benders Bandit Loot

The La Cienega (or Cieniga) Stage Station was on the Butterfield Overland Mail route near Pantano off I-10. A band of outlaws called the Benders operated the stage station. They were called the Benders as they seem to have been drunk a lot. Many murders occurred in the area, mostly done by Indians but some by the Benders. One legend claimed that they murdered a U.S. Army paymaster and took the payroll of $75,000. Shortly after the robbery, Apaches attacked the stage station and killed all the Benders.

Later, four men who called themselves prospectors were seen in the area of the old stage station looking for treasure. When they left, there were large holes remaining behind making some think they found what they were searching for. About $300 in American coins were reported to have been found in the stage station's fireplace.

Blackgown's Treasure

Spanish padres reportedly cached gold statues, chalices, bars, nuggets and gold dust in the Sierrita Mountains, about ten to fifteen miles north of Arivaca. Another version of this tale claimed that it was the third little mountain southwest to west of Tubac. See Lost Black Princess Mine/Lost Blonde Mayo Mine, as well as the Lost Vampire Bat Mine/Lost Arivaca Treasure/Lost Papago Mine.

Cienega Benders Lost Mine

Supposedly in eastern Pima County near La Cienega Stage Station. See Benders Bandit Loot, Pima County.

Colossal Cave Bandit Loot

In 1884, four bandits were said to have robbed a Southern Pacific Railroad train at the Pantano water tank stop of $62,000 in gold coins bound for Fort Lowell. When news of the robbery reached Tucson, Sheriff Bob Leatherwood organized a posse, which included Wells Fargo agents. They tracked the four robbers to Rancho de Lago, which was owned by a man named Crane. Crane was questioned and finally admitted to exchanging some of his horses for horses the four bandits had. The robbers had threatened to kill Crane if he cooperated with the lawmen. The posse tracked the four outlaws to the mouth of Colossal Cave and found Crane's four horses nearby.

The posse entered the cave but were met by gunfire from the outlaws. The posse retreated outside the cave and decided to wait for the outlaws to come out or be starved. After two weeks, nothing happened. The posse finally piled wood in front of the cave entrance and set it afire to force the outlaws out of the cave. Nothing happened.

Finally, a cowboy came with the news that four strangers in Wilcox were having a drunken celebration there. The sheriff and his posse rode to Wilcox and had a shootout with the robbers. Three robbers were killed, and outlaw Phil Carver was arrested.

Carver told the sheriff that the gang had escaped from the cave with about $2,000 through another cave entrance. They left the rest of the loot

Western saloons like this were where robbers often hung out. *Library of Congress.*

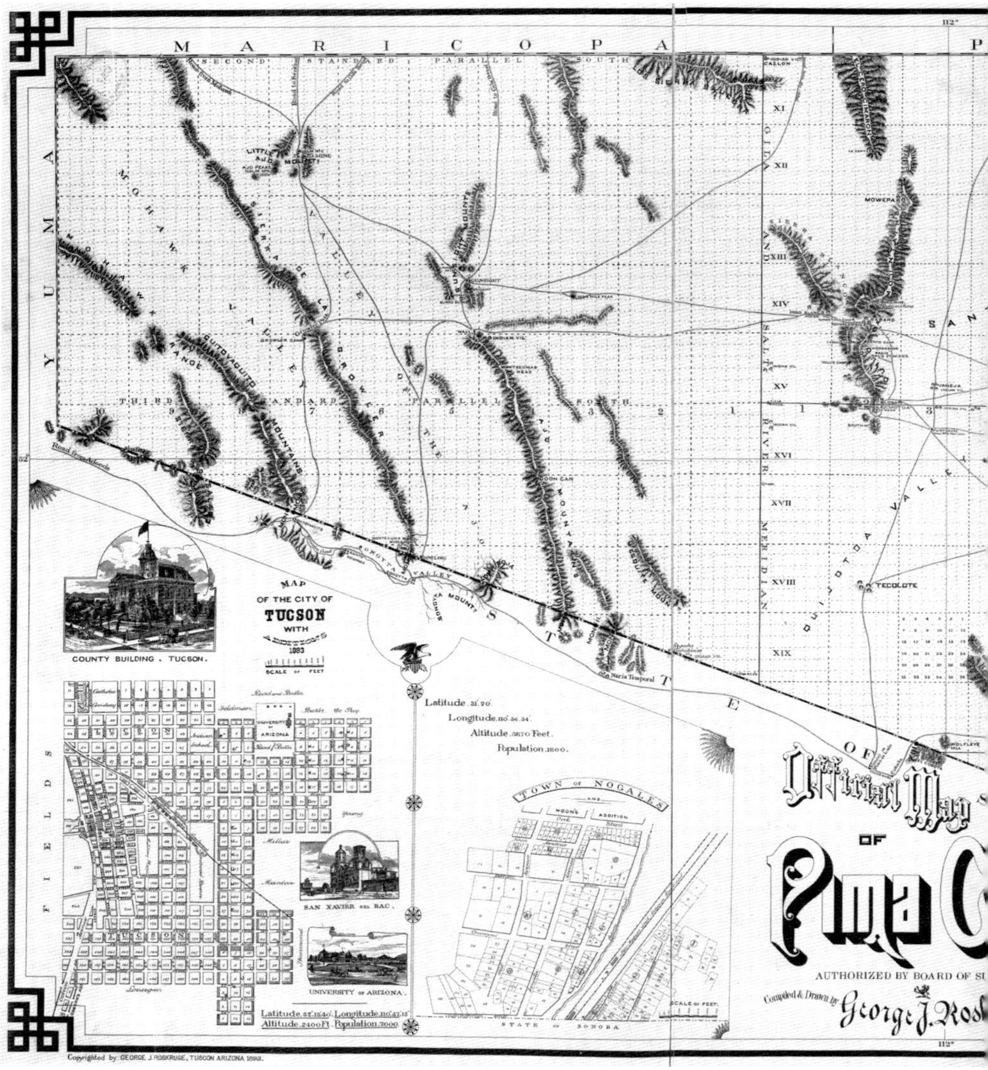

Map of Pima County in 1893 before Santa Cruz County was carved out of it. *Library of Congress.*

behind. In advance of the robbery, the gang had stocked the cave, which was then called the Hole-in-the-Wall Cave.

Carver claimed that he was just a watcher for the outlaws, but he was tried and sent to the Yuma Territorial Prison. Upon his release in 1912, he was in bad health. Wells Fargo agents trailed him, but he escaped them. It was

Sam Heintzelman and the Ortiz brothers eventually mined the site and then sold it to the Sonora Exploration and Mining Company, which was formed with $2 million in assets to develop Arizona mines. Major Sam Heintzelman was the first president of the Sonora Exploration and Mining Company and later left Arizona to serve in the U.S. Army as a major general. Arizona entrepreneur and politician Charles P. Poston was the mine superintendent and a close friend of Heintzelman's.

Raids by Indians and outlaws started when the U.S. Army left the area. In one such raid, the Heintzelman Mine lost about one hundred horses and mules. In 1861, about $70,000 worth of silver bullion was reportedly stolen from the Heintzelman Mine by its Mexican foreman, Juan (or Juanito), and a partner. Charles Poston discovered the theft. He led a posse that caught the two thieves near the Mexican border and killed both. Juan's partner admitted to the theft before dying but did not reveal where the stolen silver was cached. The silver was hidden before Juan and his partner were overtaken and killed by the posse.

Mexican bandits killed the mine supervisor's brother John Poston and eleven others in the Heintzelman Mine to steal silver and as revenge for the death of Juan and his partner. Charles Poston later became the U.S. Indian agent in Arizona Territory and had political and economic contacts that helped develop Arizona.

The Heintzelman Mine is located about twelve miles west of Arivaca Junction and west of present U.S. 89.

Jesus Arrora Treasure

On the east side of the Cocopah Mountains, Pedro Pedrillo found a rock cross with the words "dig here" in Spanish in southern Pima County. He dug out a tin box that was buried under the cross. In the box was a scroll that claimed Captain Jesus Arrora and twenty-nine men had traveled east from the wreck of the Spanish ship *Isabella Catolica* on March 29, 1682. They had discovered a rich treasure and were taking it to Mexico City when they were attacked by Indians and forced to bury it. This treasure has not been reported as being found.

John Clark's Lost Silver Mine

Miner John Clark was from Missouri and worked a rich silver vein in the Cerro Colorado Mountains from the 1850s to the beginning of the Civil War. The mine was reportedly north of Arivaca Junction, between present U.S. 286 and U.S. 89. Its silver content ran one to two ounces per ton. Clark

Panning for placer gold was possible when water was available. *New York Public Library.*

was rumored to have taken forty tons of the ore to Yuma (another version said St. Louis) to be smelted after storing forty tons of ore in the mine. Its ore supposedly sold for $80,000. He hid the mine entrance from Apaches and Sonoran bandits. He often took his ore with the Heintzelman Mine mule train carrying its ore.

Clark suddenly left the area and never returned. One version of this story claimed that he had gone to Tucson due to a hostile Indian outbreak and then went back east, where he died after enjoying his riches and telling people about his mine. It is possible that the mine was mined out or that he had enough of mining before he died. The area has been heavily mined for centuries, so it is likely it has been discovered and mined out by now.

La Virgin de Guadalupe Mine and Treasure

A legend noted that Spanish missionaries had operated La Virgin de Guadalupe Mine about eleven miles north of Arivaca Junction and two miles west of U.S. 286 in the Black Hills. A black headstone-like rock with a cross cut into it marked the mine. Rich silver ore, forty-four tons of silver bullion and a ton of gold were said to have been buried there when the Jesuits were forced out of Arizona.

Lost Ajo/Lost Carreta (Careta) Canyon Mine and Treasure

Near Arivaca and the Tascosa Mountains in the foothills. See Pinal County.

Lost Baboquivai Mountains Mine

U.S. soldiers from Fort Lowell in the 1870s chased Apaches in the Baboquivari Mountains. They stopped in a small canyon to collect water from a pool at the base of a rock ledge. Part of the group found another seasonal pool nearby, and they filled their canteens with water from it but also discovered gold nuggets in the pool. They stuffed their pockets with the nuggets before returning to chase Apaches. The soldiers never caught the Apaches. Later, two of the soldiers deserted with their horses and found the placer deposit. The pools had dried up by then. They gathered up more gold nuggets and left, but without water. Their horses collapsed and died. One of the deserters died, and the second deserter died after being found. Other soldiers reportedly searched for the placer mine, but no one reported finding it.

Lost Bean Pot Placer Mine and Treasure

There is a legend that Mexican miners were about to be attacked by Apaches, so they filled iron bean pots with their placer gold and buried them. Only a few of these miners escaped the Indian attack. The surviving miners never returned to reclaim their gold due to Indian uprisings over time. The burial site was said by some to be three miles west of present Ajo. In the 1930s, George Sears was walking and stumbled on an iron pot on the top of a hill that rolled down into the canyon. He later heard the story of the lost bean pot placer gold but did not know exactly where he had stumbled on the bean pot.

Lost Black Princess Mine/Lost Bonde Mayo Mine

Legends claim that the Lost Black Princess Mine was in the Cerro Colorado Mountains, southeast of the confluence of Altar Wash and San Juan Wash, between Baboquivari, Old Baldy (El Pelon) and Colorado Peaks. The tops of these peaks form a skyline that looks like a naked woman lying on her back when viewed from several specific locations. Opata and Papago (Tohono O'odham) Indians have legends about the Black Princess in the Cerro Colorado Mountains. In the west side of the Cerro Colorado Mountains, there was a lost Spanish mine known as the Lost Black Princess Mine. In 1751, Papago Indians revolted against the Spanish occupation of their lands. The Spanish reportedly abandoned the Black Princess Mine with its mined gold ore and wire gold.

In 1862, two Mayo Indians from southern Sonora, Juan and Fermin Morales, reportedly found this lost mine. Juan Morales was blond and called "El Guero Mayo." The Morales brothers had reportedly looked for the Lost Sapori (or Sopori) Mine. Their mine was thus called the Lost Blonde Mayo Mine. They had panned for gold along Arivaca Creek. Juan Morales discovered rich gold quartz ore. They returned from the mountains with six burros carrying gold ore. The quartz had wire gold and massive gold with a blue indigo tinge, which could have been a bromide or silver. The gold ore was weathered and oxidized with moss covering it, so it was previously mined and stockpiled a long time ago. The ore also contained porous lava rock, which could have been part of a lava pipe or chimney.

The two Morales brothers took the gold ore to Arivaca and milled it in arrastras about three miles west of Arivaca. Juan Morales always came into Arivaca from the north. It took a week for Juan Morales go to the mine and return. The mine was thought to be about eighteen to twenty miles north of Arivaca. For many months, the ore was removed from the mine and separated by the brothers.

The mine made the Morales brothers wealthy. They settled down as ranchers. Fermin Morales ran cattle on the Calera Ranch about three miles north of Arivaca. Juan Morales had a cattle ranch on Batamonte Wash below Black Princess Mountain. Juan Morales died in Mexico during a visit to the Rio Mayo Valley in Sonora in the 1930s. Fermin Morales died in Arivaca and was buried in old Camp Santo on the north edge of Arivaca. The mine was said to be near Black Woman Ridge, an area sacred to Indians. Some think that this mine could have been the Lost Sapori Mine. See Lost Sapori Mine/Treasure.

Lost Canyon of Gold

This may be in the Santa Catalina Mountains or in Pinal County.

Lost Cerro Colorado Mine

Supposedly northeast of Arivaca in the Cerro Chiquita Mountains on the south slope.

Lost Esmeralda (Emerald) Mine/La Esmeralda Church Treasure

Padre Eusebio Francisco Kino, who founded Mission San Xavier del Bac, was reportedly shown the site of green ore by an elderly Papago (Tohono O'odham) Indian in 1700. It later became known as the Esmeralda Mine. It was east of Tucson and mined by the padres. During a Papago and Pima revolt in 1723, gold bars and church ornaments were hidden at the Esmeralda Mine. When the revolt ended, the treasure and church ornaments were returned to the mission. During another Papago and Pima Indian revolt in 1751, gold and church ornaments were again hidden at the mine until the Indian uprising ended and then were returned to the mission. With the expulsion of the Jesuit padres in 1767, the mission padres were said to again have hidden their gold and church ornaments in the mine. Once again, the treasure was returned to the mission when the new priests arrived to take over the mission.

In 1822, all the Spanish priests were expelled from Mission San Xavier del Bac by the Mexican government. The mission church treasure was said to have been taken once more to the mine and hidden. The Esmeralda Mine was about six miles southeast of Mission San Xavier del Bac, along the southern Santa Catalina Mountains ridge. Mission Indian descendants have also said that the Esmeralda Mine was southwest of the mission in the Sierrita Mountains. See Lost Treasure of Mission San Xavier del Bac.

Lost Fortune (Fortuna) Mine

Said to be a few hours' journey east of Tucson. This could be in Cochise County.

Lost Jabonero (Soapmaker) Mine

There are several versions of this story, written by Harold O. Wright, John Mitchell, Roscoe Wilson and others. In 1849–50, when this part of Arizona was part of Mexico, two Mexican miners on El Camino del Diablo (the Devil's Road) traveled from Tinajas Altas to Tule Tank en route to Sonoyta, Mexico. They camped for the night, but one horse wandered away. One of the men tracked it and found a hill covered with gold nuggets. He rejoined his comrade in Sonoyta, and they told a jabonero (soapmaker) there about their discovery. They made the soapmaker a partner, with him supplying supplies and pack animals to mine the gold. All three left for the mine but were attacked on the way by Papago Indians, who killed the two miners. The surviving soapmaker was never able to find the lost mine but gave a statement or waybill on September 27, 1878, giving directions to the lost mine.

Lost Medicine Man Gold Mine

Rumored to be in the Ajo area.

Lost Mine of fhe Ajo Mountains

Located in western Pima County, according to legend.

Lost Mine with the Iron Door/Lost Escalante Mine
See Pinal County.

Lost Orphan Mine
This may be in the Cabeza Prieta Mountains near Tule Tank.

Lost Padillo Gold Mine
Said to be near Arivaca.

Lost Papago Indian Mine
A Papago Indian mined gold about three miles east of an Indian village, which was said to have been about fifty miles east of Ajo. On his deathbed, he told his son where his gold mine was located. The mine entrance was hidden behind a rock slab and brush in the Santa Rosa Mountains near a limestone depression that often filled with rainwater that dried up. He reportedly averaged about $130 per burro load.

Lost San Pedro Mine/La Mina Del San Pedro
See Santa Cruz County.

Lost Sapori Mine/Treasure
The Spanish were said to have discovered a gold and silver deposit located in either Arizona or Sonora that became known as the Sapori Mine. The Sapori Mine was lost and then later found. Some say it was on the twenty-one-thousand-acre Sapori (Sopori) Ranch and land grant in southern Pima

Baboquivari Mountain is a topographical marker for several lost mines. *John and Bev Passarello.*

County. Early maps located it in the northern part of the Cerro Colorado Mountains. One story was that gold ore was smelted in an arroyo west of the Black Princess Mountain. An old mission attached to the mine was said to be in the Altos Valley east of Baboquivari Peak. This may have been a *visita* or mission occasionally attended to by padres.

One story has the rich vein ending and that this is the reason the mine was abandoned. Another story claimed that gold and silver from the mine were buried in the corner of an adobe house on the old ranch where the Sapori mineworkers lived. This sounds like the Arivaca Treasure in Arivaca. Apache raids were common, and that's likely why the mine was abandoned. There was some confusion between the Sapori Mine and the Isabelle Mine. The Isabelle Mine was said to have been about 1.5 miles south of the Sapori Ranch house and was worked by padres from Tumacacori Mission. Some think that this lost mine is also the Lost Black Princess Mine. This could be in Santa Cruz County. See the Lost Black Princess Mine/Lost Blonde Mayo Mine, as well as Arivaca Treasure.

LOST SHEPHERD MINE AND TREASURE

De Estine Shepherd's lost mine and treasure of gold ore and bullion (worth $5 million) was said to be southwest of Arivaca. While ill just after Christmas 1905 in the hospital, Shepherd married the boardinghouse owner with whom he had been staying. He wanted to give her the secret location of his mine. Shepherd had worked his mine for twenty years. He told her that the map to his mine was with a friend in Tucson. After Shepherd died, she went to Tucson and discovered that the friend had moved to Mexico. She tracked his friend down in Mexico and learned that the friend had sent the trunk containing the map to Omaha, Nebraska. She and her new husband searched for the trunk and discovered that it had been sold as unclaimed freight. They found the buyer, who claimed that he had destroyed the map and papers in the trunk. She searched for the mine but never found it.

LOST SPOON GOLD MINE

Said to be located between Tucson and Arivaca.

LOST TENHACHAPE MINE

This could be in southwestern Pima County.

LOST TREASURE OF MISSION SAN XAVIER DEL BAC

A legend said that the altar of Mission San Xavier del Bac was estimated to be worth more than $60,000 in 1860 when miners reported seeing the old mission's treasures. When the Civil War broke out, Union soldiers were withdrawn from the Arizona Territory. Without the American military garrisons, Apaches started raiding mines and ranches in the area. The Treasure of Mission San Xavier Del Bac suddenly disappeared. Indians from the area claimed that the treasure was buried among the tailings and workings of the Esmeralda Mine. See Lost Esmeralda (Emerald) Mine/La Esmeralda Church Treasure.

Lost Vampire Bat Mine/Lost Arivaca Treasure/Lost Pagago Mine

A lost Spanish mine with gold nuggets was said to be located in the eastern Baboquivari Mountains, southwest of Tucson. The Baboquivari Mountains are mostly on the eastern edge of the Tohono O'odham Indian Reservation, which was formerly called the Papago Indian Reservation. This mine and treasure located near Arivaca were estimated to be worth $400,000 in gold ore and gold ingots hidden by Spanish padres. The old Spanish settlement was located a few miles upstream of Arivaca Creek from the present town of Arivaca, which is one of the oldest Spanish settlements in Arizona.

A Papago Indian was said to have found the treasure in the 1870s or about 1880. The man was tracking a wounded deer on Baboquivari Mountain's eastern slope. He was on a long ridge running northerly from Baboquivari Mountain when he saw vampire bats exiting from an old mine entrance. He went inside the old mine and said that there were hundreds of gold and silver bars inside, possibly from the late 1600s and hidden by Jesuits. Along the old mine's walls were rotted buckskin bags of gold nuggets. The nuggets would indicate that this gold came from placer deposits.

The mine was located west of Arivaca. The Papago Indian took one sack of nuggets to purchase supplies from an Arivaca area trading post. When he was an old man, some miners threatened the Papago with harm if he would not lead them to the mine. The Indian had a new home on Arivaca Creek. The old Indian told the men or the trading post worker that the mine was on a ridge that was northeast from Baboquivari Peak toward Tucson. The men went into the mountains but did not see any bats exiting from a cave or mine. Before the Papago Indian died, he said that he covered up the mine entrance with the bats inside to hide it after taking out enough gold to meet his needs.

Mexican Bandit Loot

A Mexican bandit gang crossed into Arizona near Sasabe after robbing towns in northern Mexico. The bandits camped in the nearby mountains. At the time, there was unrest along the U.S./Mexico border, so U.S. troops were actively hunting bandits. On September 30, 1913, U.S. soldiers attacked the bandits and reportedly killed all but one. Before dying two days later, the bandit claimed that the gang had buried their loot at a place where you could see the town of Sasabe to the west—you could also go to the other side of the hill on the north slope and look down Arivaca's main street.

Mexican Gold

When southern Arizona was part of Mexico, Papago Indians sometimes picked up gold nuggets to trade for supplies. Some Mexican miners learned where the Papagos were finding the gold and moved in on the placer deposit. The Mexican miners were very successful in recovering gold, which they stored in a large earthenware pot called an olla. Apaches attacked the Mexican miners. The legend claimed that the miners buried the olla full of gold as they fought the Apaches. A number of the miners were killed during the battle. The survivors fled from the area.

The Papagos were afraid that the Apaches would stay in the area, so they asked their medicine man to cast a spell to drive them away. The medicine man took some white dust from a buckskin bag he had hanging on his neck and cast a spell. A sandstorm hit the area and was said to have driven the Apaches away and left the treasure hidden.

Mission San Jose del Tucson Treasure

In about 1775, Padre Francisco Tomas Carces built a mission, San Jose del Tucson, just two miles south of the pueblo of Tucson. This mission was later abandoned, and Mission San Xavier del Bac became the primary mission in the region. Treasure from Mission San Jose del Tucson was said to have been hidden near or in the old mission. Early pioneers dug in the old mission garden looking for Spanish treasure, but only one old Spanish coin was reportedly found.

Mission San Marcelo Treasure/Sonoyta Mine

Mission San Marcelo was located about a mile northeast of Lukeville near the Mexican border. The mission was first established in 1699 by Padre Eusebio Kino and built by Jesuit Padre Miguel Diaz from 1733 to 1735. Padre Diaz helped the mission prosper. Silver and gold ingots were said to have been smelted and hidden there. In 1751, a Papago Indian revolt killed Padre Diaz and two priests. The Papagos had been used as slaves to mine gold and silver for the mission. The Papagos destroyed the mission and

Spanish mines. Treasure was supposedly buried nearby in a mine, with a rock slab containing an iron ring sealing the entrance.

A Spanish mine operated by Mission San Barcelo at Sonoyta, Mexico, was reported to be located east of Fable Mountain. Mission San Barcelo in Mexico was destroyed during the Pima Revolt of 1751, when Padre Enrique Ruhen and several Indians were killed.

Another version of the tale said that Padre Diaz and the two other murdered priests were put in an underground room with their silver and gold. The room's roof and walls were caved in. The rich mine the padres got gold from was from the Santa Lucia Mine in the Pozo Redondo Mountains. During the Papago revolt of 1751, the treasure was moved to hiding places in the Arizona mountains. One of the locations where the gold and silver was possibly hidden is the southwestern part of Pima County in a Puerto Blanco Mountains cave. The gold and silver were stored at Mission San Marcelo, which was located about one mile north of Sonoyta, Sonora, Mexico. Another location the gold and silver were said to be hidden was in a Tortilla Mountains cave in southeastern Pinal County.

Montezuma's Head Treasure

Legends claimed that another treasure from the Aztec ruler Montezuma, worth about $1.5 million in gold ore and bullion (or $1 million to $2 million in gold bars, fifty bags of gold bullion and thirty bags of gold nuggets), was buried in a cave near Montezuma's Head in the Estrella Mountains. One version indicates that the treasure was halfway between Butterfly Peak and Montezuma's Head. Other possible locations were in the Ajo Mountains or near Tucson.

Patrick O'Donahue Treasure

Irish adventurer Patrick O'Donahue became known as Pedriac Odonoju when he settled down in Spanish territories. O'Donahue had resisted the English occupation of Ireland. He left his native Ireland for Spanish Catholic lands. He became a loyal soldier for the Spanish king. He was rewarded for his service to the Spanish Crown with a sixty-thousand-acre land grant. His land grant was in the southwestern area of Pima County and consisted of twelve leagues in Papagueria or Papago country.

O'Donahue built a hacienda and a mission in the Altar Valley that was called the Four Evangelists. He called his land the Garden of Solitude. He provided shelter for travelers, be they Spanish or Indian, and was well thought of by the Papagos. One day in 1780, Apaches attacked his hacienda, killed everyone and burned the hacienda to the ground. O'Donahue was said to have hidden his treasure, which included gold nuggets given to him by Papagos. The hacienda was thought to have been located near Papago Well, west of Organ Pipe National Monument, but could also possibly be in Mexico.

Red Rock Treasure

A legend claimed that a cave between Red Rock Butte and the Silver Bell Mountains contained gold and silver that had been given by Papago Indians to a group of white men before the Spanish arrived. A raid by other Indians killed all the white people. The Papagos sealed off the cave with the treasure, as they thought it was cursed.

Rincon Mountains Gold

A party of Spanish padres and mission Indians were looking for a place to establish a ranchería in the Rincon Mountains southeast of Tucson, when they were said to have discovered a rich gold deposit. They mined the gold and were returning to Sonora when they were attacked by Apaches in the lower part of the Rincon Mountains. The Apaches captured the party's horses, including the ones packing the gold. The Spanish and mission Indians suffered few losses during the attack but had to walk back to Sonora empty-handed. The Apaches reportedly hid the captured gold in a mountain cave, which may be in the Saguaro National Park area.

Pinal County

Lost Canyon of Gold

See Pima County.

Lost Cinnabar Deposit

A lost cinnabar deposit near Casa Grande was supposedly used by Indians to paint their bodies red. In 1697, Juan Mateo Munje searched for the cinnabar mine. Mercury from cinnabar was a vital ingredient in extracting gold from its ore and was very prized by Spanish miners.

LOST MINE WITH THE IRON DOOR/LOST ESCALANTE MINE

The Escalante Mine was said to have been found in the 1760s by Padre Juan Bautista de Escalante. The mine was located in the Santa Catalina Mountains northeast of Tucson. Padre Escalante's gold was used in his mission. The Jesuits worked the mine with Papago Indians until the Jesuits were expelled by the Spanish in 1767.

One tale about the Escalante Mines was that the miners were celebrating San Juan's Day in June 1769 (or 1796), when Apaches attacked and killed many miners. The gold ore and bullion had been placed in a vault or a cave protected by an iron door. The padres and surviving miners fled south to the safety of Sonora. The Escalante Mine was reportedly a mine or a cave with a vault near the south bank of the Cañon del Oro (Canyon of Gold), about one league northwest of a hole in a rock or window (*ventana*). The old camp and chapel ruins were near the Santa Catalina Mountains, south of Oracle or between Tucson and Oracle.

Colonel Antonio Narbona led a Mexican expedition against Apaches and found gold nuggets in the Cañon del Oro on June 29, 1843. Some believe that the nuggets indicated that mining for gold had previously occurred there and that this was the site of the Lost Escalante Mine.

The Lost Escalante Mine was reportedly one of the richest Jesuit mines. One Escalante Mine location was supposed to be about twelve miles northeast of Tucson. A 1923 novel, *The Mine with the Iron Door*, written by Harold Bell Wright, was based on the Escalante Mine legend. Wright's novel was made into a silent movie in 1924 and a talkie in 1936. Wright lived for a while in Tucson and was a prolific writer. Could be in Pima County.

Several lost mines are in the Santa Catalina Mountains area. *John and Bev Passarello.*

Lost Peralta Mine
See Maricopa County.

Lost Two Ex-Soldiers Mine
Two U.S. Army soldiers were discharged at Fort McDowell. They both went prospecting in the Superstition Mountains. They were unsuccessful. They fired at a deer but missed, hitting a rock ledge instead. They inspected the ledge and picked up ore knocked off from the ledge. They later both went to work as miners in the Silver King Mine. The mine foreman, Jack Frazier, saw the ore samples and told them that the samples were rich in gold. Frazier agreed to grubstake the two men for 50 percent of their mine. Frazier set up a $500 line of credit at the Silver King store for them. The two former soldiers drew $265 in supplies and left for their mine but never returned. Later, two skeletons were found in the Superstition Mountains that many thought were these two men. One rumor was that a gambler named Smith followed them and killed them for the mine. Smith was said to have become rich and moved to Alaska.

Lost Wagoner Mine
See Maricopa County.

Mission San Marcelo Treasure
See Pima County.

Montezuma Treasure
Some Aztec treasure was hidden from the Spanish conquistadors when Montezuma was killed. One rumored cached treasure was at the Casa Grande National Monument ruins, about nine miles west of Florence. Casa Grande was a four-story building constructed in about 1320 by the Hohokam Indians and abandoned before 1450. It may have been used as an astronomy observatory.

Picacho Peak Treasure
After sacking the Spanish missions and towns, the Yuma Indians were said to have transported gold to the base of Picacho Peak (also called Squaw Peak and Sugarloaf) in Picacho Peak State Park. See Sunlit Cave Treasure, La Paz County and Mission La Purísima Concepción and Mission Bicuner Treasures, Yuma County.

Spanish treasure was reportedly hidden near Picacho Peak. *John and Bev Passarello.*

Wagon Train Treasure

A wagon train headed for the California gold fields in about 1850 was said to have carried $50,000 in a chest or iron pot, which they buried every night when they camped and circled the wagons. Near Montezuma's Head in Organ Pipe Cactus National Monument area, the wagon train was attacked early one morning by Apaches. Everyone in the wagon train was killed. The wagons were looted and burned. One of the families who had left the wagon train before it was attacked told the story of the gold and silver cache being made every night.

Yuma's Lost Mine

Lieutenant Thomas "Buffalo Tom" McLean (or McLain) was reportedly a West Point Military Academy graduate who served as acting U.S. Army quartermaster at Fort Yuma, California. Fort Yuma guarded the Colorado River crossing connecting California and Arizona Territory. McLean was involved in an army contracting scandal. He was charged, court-martialed and discharged from the U.S. Army in disgrace. "Going Indian," Lieutenant McLean married a Yuma Indian chief's daughter and was called "Yuma."

In spite of being a white man and former soldier, Yuma was trusted by the Yuma, Papago and Apache Indian tribes near Fort Yuma. Yuma traded with Indians by supplying them with guns, ammunition, cloth and other trading items from Yuma and Tucson, Arizona Territory.

Yuma learned that Aravaipa Apaches had a secret gold placer mine. They traded placer gold for trade goods. This group had an Aravaipa Apache ranchería, or town, about five miles from Camp Grant at the junction of the San Pedro River and Aravaipa Creek, just a few miles southwest of the current town of Winkleman. Camp Grant was a U.S. Army military post established in 1860.

One Aravaipa Apache whom Yuma traded with was Chief Es-kim-en-zin. In about 1860, after much effort, Yuma persuaded Chief Es-kim-en-zin to show him the location of the Apaches' hidden placer gold mine. They rode northwest from the Aravaipa Apache camp near Camp Grant up a rocky ridge and then along its crest for three miles. They came to a mountain range overlooking the San Pedro Valley to the east. After reportedly riding north for about six miles, they halted at a depression in the ground. Chief Es-kim-en-zin dug a rock sample from the ground, gave it to Yuma and left. This rock was full of gold.

Yuma returned to his trading post and enlisted the help of General Walker (probably Joseph R. Walker or John Walker) as a partner in the gold mine. General Walker was likely the fur trapper Joe Walker, who was famous for prospecting and exploration. Walker had discovered rich gold placer mines up the Hassayampa River. Yuma guided his partner Walker to the hidden Apache mine. The two dug up several saddlebags of the gold-sprinkled rock and took them to Tucson. By 1861, the U.S. military had been mostly withdrawn from Arizona due to the start of the American Civil War. The Apaches attacked mines, raided cabins and attacked small settlements throughout Arizona Territory.

Due to the Apache attacks, Yuma gathered his stock and trading goods to move them to a safer area. The Papago Indians believed that Yuma was on the side of their enemies, the Apaches, since he often traded with the Apaches. A group of Papago warriors crept into Yuma's camp one night, attacked him with clubs and killed him while he slept.

An Apache uprising caused Joe Walker to abandon the rich mine. The hostile Apaches killed many American and Mexican miners and settlers. Eventually, Union troops from California arrived to put down the uprising and restored communication between California and the East. Before dying from tuberculosis in 1865 as peace returned to Arizona, Walker told his friend John Sweeney where Yuma's mine was located. Sweeney did not go prospecting in Apache country to look for the lost gold mine. Sweeney preferred to get drunk and tell stories. Sweeney reportedly told Charles O. Brown where the mine was located. Brown searched for the mine but never found it.

Another version of Yuma's lost gold was that Yuma's partner was freighter John J. Crittenden (not Joe Walker). Crittenden also hauled freight between

Fort Yuma and Tucson. Yuma and Crittenden went together to the rich placer mine (or lode mine). They dug up gold for a few hours and took the gold to Tucson, where they sold thirty pounds of the gold for $1,200 (or $12,000 by another tale). This equates to $51,000 per ton. Yuma and Crittenden were trailed into the desert and mountains by other miners and prospectors in the Tucson area who wanted to know where the rich mine was. They knew where there was a new gold discovery, there would be other gold deposits nearby.

A band of Papago Indians murdered Yuma and his wife on a trading trip. Only Crittenden knew where the rich gold placer was located. Eventually, Crittenden believed that it was safe to return to the mine to get some more gold. He left Camp Grant and claimed that he was just going hunting. He was never seen or heard from again. His camp was found by the U.S. cavalry, but Crittenden was not found. The people at Camp Grant figured that Yavapai Apaches murdered Crittenden.

Americans in the Camp Grant area encouraged Papago Indians and Mexicans to seek revenge against the Apaches for their raids. On April 30, 1871, a group of Papagos and Mexicans stormed the Aravaipa Apache camp near Camp Grant. About 85 to 135 Aravaipa Apaches were murdered, and this band was essentially wiped out. Most of the Apaches murdered were women and children. The location of the lost Aravaipa Apache gold mine called Yuma's Lost Mine remains lost to this day.

Santa Cruz County

John Ward's Cache

Prospector John Ward reportedly hid gold coins at or near his adobe home west of Patagonia.

Lost Ajo Treasure/Lost Carretta (Careta) Canyon Mine and Treasure

The Lost Ajo Treasure or Lost Carretta (Careta) Canyon Treasure was said to have been a mine, mint and storage area for Jesuits on a cart trail called the old Carretta Road or El Camino. This trail was on the west bank of the Santa Cruz River below Tubac and connected Mission Tumacacori and Mission San Barcelo at Sonoyta, Mexico. The treasure was rumored to have been $1 million to $2 million in gold bars, silver bars and ore, along with church treasures. Spanish missionaries fled the mission at Altar, Mexico, with their treasure during the 1751 Pima uprising. Eight mules were said to have carried mission treasure bound for Mission Tumacacori.

A group coming from Mission Tumacacori with that mission's treasure met the caravan and reported that Mission Tumacacori had already been attacked by Indians and destroyed. The treasure from both missions was reportedly hidden in a nearby mine. The treasure and lost Spanish silver mine were said to have been in the Atasco Mountains, about six miles south and four miles east of Arivaca. One of the items hidden was the Mission Tumacacori records, along with a map indicating the location of eight Spanish mines near Mission Tumacacori. See Pima County.

Lost La Purísima Concepción Mine/Treasure

A legend indicated that Spanish padres had a gold and silver mine about ten to fifteen miles south of Tumacacori Mission in the Pajarito Mountains. Also, two other rumored mines were fifteen miles southwest of Mission Tumacacori. One mine was slightly south of the Cerro El Ruido Mountain or Noisy Mountain in the Pajarito Mountains, but it could be in Mexico. Some claimed that they heard thunder or pipe organ sounds coming from the mountain. A lost mission with a storeroom of silver hidden in a cave was reportedly in the area.

Some said that the treasure left behind was worth $15 million. The ore consisted of about 50 percent silver and 20 percent gold, reportedly $472,000 per ton. Directions in some publications for one mine were to take

The Santa Cruz River Valley was a vital route for pack trains between Tucson and Sonora. *John and Bev Passarello.*

State Highway 289 four miles west of Calabasas along Calabasas Canyon and look for a narrow pass through a tributary canyon on the north side with a big caliche and kaolin deposit. The mine was along the face of the deposit. The white kaolin clay supposedly contained silver and gold nodules from small nuggets to coconut-sized nuggets. This lost mine was rumored to have been found and lost several times by a number of people.

At the beginning of the twentieth century, a prospector brought two burro loads of silver nodules covered by clay to Nogales. He claimed he found them in El Ruido Mountains near two old Spanish arrastras next to a creek. This prospector died while celebrating his find, and the mine was again lost.

Lost Opata Silver Mine

Spaniards supposedly operated a rich silver mine until it was abandoned and hidden in 1766. Although the Opata Indians resisted Spanish occupation, they were used as slave labor to mine the rich ore there. The mine was said to have had a tunnel in the side of the mountain. The ore was crushed and refined into bars and stored in a large room in the mine. There was a story that the Opatas kidnapped a Mayo Indian woman and later sacrificed her in the mine. The padres were said to have abandoned silver in the mine and had the Indians fill up the tunnel to hide it. The Opatas then returned to their homes in Sonora.

In 1914, an old Opata Indian was reworking this old mine. Writer John Mitchell reported seeing five sacks of silver ore from the mine in 1915 and examined the mine in the western foothills of the San Cayetano Mountains. This mine was said to be about five miles south of Mission San Cayetano de Tumacacori in the western hills of the San Cayetano Mountains. This sounds a lot like the Sycamore Canyon mine story except for the location. See Sycamore Canyon/San Ignacio Mine/Geronimo's Lost Mine, Yavapai County.

Lost Planchas de Plata Mine

This could be in southern Santa Cruz County.

Lost San Pedro Mine/La Mina del San Pedro

The Spanish reportedly worked the San Pedro Mine until 1648. It was as one of a number of Mission Tumacacori silver mines. The mine was said to have been on the eastern slope of the Atasco Mountains and could be in Pima County. Jesuit padres sealed the mine before leaving in 1767. The lost mine was four to five miles due west of the Mission Tumacacori or the Tubac Presidio.

The ore averaged $4,000 per ton. Mined silver was also hidden in the mine. One way to find the mine is to be there at sunrise. As the sun rises over the Santa Rita Mountains to the east, the sun was supposed to shine directly into the mine tunnel.

Lost Sapori Mine/Treasure

See Pima County.

Lost Spanish Silver Mine

A lost Spanish silver mine near Tumacacori was rumored to be about half a mile north of Sonita Creek and about a mile east of the Santa Cruz River. It was abandoned in 1772 by the Spanish due to Apache Indian raids. Two Opata Indians reportedly found the mine in the 1920s and mined it until they died. Some suggest that they were high grading on private property and using the mine story as a cover.

Lost Spanish Treasure

A lost Spanish treasure was supposedly buried in a cliff rock shelter under rocks at Camp Loco. It was on an old trail leading from Mission San Xavier del Bac, about eight miles north of Patagonia.

Lost Tumacacori Mine

Said to be in western Santa Cruz County in the Tumacacori Mountains. A prospector brought in a fist-sized ore sample into John Connors's saloon in Nogales and claimed that he bought the ore sample from an Opata Indian. The Indian claimed that he found it along Carrizo Creek while out hunting. Connors grubstaked the prospector, who died shortly thereafter from drinking and the elements.

Lost Virgin de Guadalupe Silver Mine/Treasure

A Spanish mine was rumored to have been located about four miles southwest of Mission Tumacacori in the Tumacacori Mountains or Santa Rita Mountains, as well as just north of the San Ramon River near Tubac. Some sources claimed that it was 1,800 yards north of Mission Tumacacori. The mine was in porphyry rock angled down between two peaks. A black headstone-shaped rock with a chiseled cross was on the east face. The Spaniards worked the mine in about 1648, and Mexican miners later also

A lost mine was said to be near Carrizo Creek. *New York Public Library.*

worked the mine. The mine entrance was then hidden. Mission Tumacacori was founded in 1691 as Mission San Jose de Tumacacori.

Another version of the story has it that near the mine there was a rock with "CCB/TD" carved on it. South of the carved stone was a marker of rocks over the hidden mine entrance. In 1751, Pima Indians revolted and destroyed Mission Tumacacori, chasing the Spanish away. In 1767, the Jesuits were expelled and were rumored to have hidden 2,050 mule loads of silver and 205 mule loads of gold worth $25 million in the mine tunnel. The Franciscans then came and took over the mission.

The present Mission Tumacacori was built in 1822 and abandoned in 1848. These mission ruins are visible today. See Mission Tumacacori Treasure, Santa Cruz County.

MISSION GUEVAVI TREASURE AND LOST MINE

About twelve miles north of Mission Tumacacori, there was a small mission, Mission San Gabriel de Guevavi. Just north of Mission San Gabriel de Guevavi at Calabasas, Jesuit padres were rumored to have buried mission treasures and several hundred bars of bullion from their mine. The day before the Pima Indians destroyed Mission Guevavi in 1695, two tons of church treasure were supposedly hidden in a nearby mine. The treasure consisted of gold and silver crucifixes, chalices, a monstrance, a ciborium, a baldachin, candelabras and *lamparas de aceite*.

There was a story that the bells at Mission Guevavi were also hidden at the mission. The mission bells were cast from heavy black silver-copper ore from a site north of the mission in the southwestern San Cayetano Mountains. Treasure hunters over the years have destroyed much of the mission's ruins looking for the treasure. The site of the mission is northeast of Nogales and southwest of the San Cayetano Mountains. Pima Indians revolted in 1751 and plundered Mission San Gabriel de Guevavi de Calabasas. Jesuits worked the mine and reportedly abandoned a large quantity of platinum, which was then considered to be worthless.

A Nogales woodcutter, Juan Bustamonte, spent summers in the mountains prospecting when there was no demand for his wood. In about 1917, Bustamonte found an ancient wooden cross and the entrance to an old mine. People noticed that instead of bringing small amounts of gold dust from his mountain trips, he brought back two mule loads of silver ore. He and a friend later took other burro loads of silver ore from the mountains. A storm later blocked the route to the mine, ending his trips. Bustamonte died sometime in the 1970s. He had told his friends that the church treasure was deep inside the silver mine. It may be located up a rocky canyon on the southwestern slopes of the Cayetano Mountains about six miles northeast of Nogales. See Lost Virgin de Guadalupe Silver Mine/Treasure, Santa Cruz County.

MISSION TUMACACORI TREASURE

Pima Indians invited Padre Eusebio Francisco Kino to visit their Tumacacori village in 1691. In 1696, Padre Estubio Kino founded Mission San Jose de Tumacacori, which was originally called Mission San Cayetano de Tumacacori. Mission Tumacacori was originally established on the west bank of the Santa Cruz River. The present mission site is on the east bank of the Santa Cruz River and is part of the Tumacacori National Historic Park. Franciscan Padre Nacisco Gutierrez began the present church in 1794, but it was never completely finished. After Mexico became independent, the padres abandoned the mission between 1849 and 1853 because of Apache raids. Four church bells were said to have been hidden within easy walking distance from the church by two padres. One bell was dated 1809. Some stories indicated that the bells were made of silver, but in 1849, H.M.T. Powell noted that the bells were made of copper, tin and iron.

In about 1902, a man brought two bell clappers to the University of Arizona. He thought that they were part of the lost mission bells. The man's grandfather found them in a field near the mission. Another story

Mission Tumacacori was surrounded by old Spanish and Mexican mines. *John and Bev Passarello.*

said that the bells were mostly copper and were melted down for their gold and silver content. A tunnel was rumored to have led from the old mission on the west bank of the Santa Cruz River bank, with a Spanish treasure hidden in the tunnel.

PETE KITCHEN RANCH CACHE

A $20,000 cache of gold coins (or forty thousand pesos) was rumored to be hidden on the Pete Kitchen Ranch near Nogales. This cache represented the proceeds of several cattle sales. It was said to have been buried in a lard can under a tree. Pete Kitchen was an early pioneer rancher who stayed and defended his ranch during Apache uprisings in the area when others fled. A Mexican woman and two men asked a later ranch owner for permission to search his ranch for the treasure, but they never found it.

PIEDRA BLANCA TREASURE

Apaches living at Las Lagunas, the site of the Pete Kitchen Ranch, were said to have attacked a Spanish pack train of burros carrying gold and silver heading for Mexico. The Apaches hid the loot under a *piedra blanca* (white rock). The Spaniards retaliated and wiped out most of the Apaches. Three Apaches escaped and told this tale but never returned to recover the treasure. This treasure cache was supposed to have been hidden near Nogales.

VALVERDES GOLD

The old Spanish Valverdes family settled in the Santa Cruz Valley near Mission San Gabriel de Guevavi (also called San Rafael and San Miguel). They were ranchers who found a rich gold mine in the mountains. The Valverdes reportedly built a stone vault under the main ranch house to store their mined gold. Once a year, a large Valverdes pack train carried their gold south to Mexico.

During the Primeria Alta Revolt in 1772, the Indians attacked and burned Spanish ranches and settlements throughout the region. The Valverdes family fled south and reportedly abandoned their gold, cattle and horses. The Valverdes were said to have remained in Mexico, where they enjoyed the wealth they had sent there. Due to Indian hostility, they never returned to their ranch.

Yavapai County

De Espejo's Mine

In 1583, Spaniard Antonio de Espejo led an expedition into what is now New Mexico and Arizona looking for three missing padres, as well as rumored gold and silver. Antonio de Espejo was a wealthy mining engineer expanding his reach into the Spanish borderlands. He later became the governor of Spanish New Mexico.

Espejo's men found huge copper deposits in south central Coconino County. They mined ore samples, made maps of the location and sent the samples and maps to Mexico City.

Spanish authorities sent another expedition from Mexico to verify the rich find. This expedition reportedly found a gold mine. Spanish soldiers and about two hundred Opata Indians were reportedly sent from Mexico in about 1720 and opened a gold mining camp. The Indians were slaves who mined the gold ore. The gold ore was refined on site, stored and then transported back to Mexico. In about 1760, the mine was reportedly abandoned.

Historian Bancroft thought that De Espejo's mine was near Bill Williams Mountain just south of Williams. Another possible location is Sycamore Canyon, between Jerome and Perkinsville. In spite of the stories that this was a gold mine, it could have been a copper or silver mine. Another location mentioned for this lost mine is in the Santa Maria Mountains, near where Walnut Creek joins Chino Creek. See Sycamore Canyon/San Ignacio Mine/Geronimo's Lost Mine.

Harper's Lost Gold Mine

Chalmer Harper's lost mine was said to be near Prescott in the Smith Canyon area of the Juniper Mountains.

Lost Black Mesa Gold Mine

Reportedly located in the Bradshaw Mountains, west of Black Creek and Arrastre Creek in Black Canyon at the base of Black Mesa.

Lost Brown and Davis Pick Mine and Treasure

In about 1871, prospectors Brown and Davis found an eighteen-inch quartz vein containing gold after following an Apache from a Phoenix store where the Apache had traded gold for goods. The two men built an arrastra at a spring to process the ore. A group of Apaches killed Davis, but Brown escaped. They left a pick at the vein. Brown returned to Arizona when he was about eighty. Brown got sick and died, but before dying, he disclosed this tale. A Mexican goat herder was said to have later found the pick but had not heard this story. The goat herder was unable to relocate where he had seen the pick.

Some $80,000 in amalgam gold was supposedly cached between a large boulder and white volcanic ash outcrops along a little valley along the mountains on the east side of a small valley in Bronco Canyon, about four miles east of Bumblebee.

Lost Coconino Mine

See Coconino County.

Lost Lord Dupa Mine

See Maricopa County.

Lost Mine of the Gold Cup

May be near Congress Junction.

Lost Negro Ben Mine

Negro Ben had worked for Major Peeples at his Peeples Valley Ranch. An Apache showed him the general location of a gold ore deposit near Antelope Peak, east of Congress Junction. Eventually, Negro Ben found the ore deposit and mined enough of it to go to Wickenburg and spend it. When he ran out of drinking money, he would return to his mine. He always left Wickenburg and headed west toward the Harquahala Mountains. He would always return to town from the same direction. Many thought that his mine was not west but north of Wickenburg near Oro Grande. Negro Ben was eventually killed by Apaches and was found four miles north of Wickenburg. Some thought that the mine was near McCraken or northeast of Wickenburg, maybe in the south end of Peeples Valley. Gold finders Major Peeples and Ed Schieffelin looked for Negro Ben's mine without success.

Lost Organ Grinder Mine

In the early 1860s, a story claimed that three Italian organ grinders were on a trail when they discovered a Mohave Indian dying of thirst. They gave the man water. As a reward, he supposedly told them the location of a rich deposit of gold and guided them there. They traveled to a canyon west of Prescott, north of Peoples Canyon and north of Congress Junction, where they found a rich ledge of chocolate-colored rock full of gold. They mined some gold and headed off for supplies. A party of Hualapai Indians attacked them, and only one organ grinder (who was away from the other prospectors) escaped death. He headed for Wickenburg carrying a canteen of water but was burdened down with rich gold ore. After a few days, a teamster named Francisco Gonzales found the dying man, who told him about their rich discovery before he died.

Lost Squaw Hollow Gold Ledge
See Maricopa County.

Lost Stoker Mine
Said to be in the Yarnell area.

Lost Tonto Apache Mine
See Coconino County.

Lost Wheel Mine
May be near Cordes and Mayer.

Major Peeples's Lost Mine
During the Civil War, Indians brought gold into La Paz and other towns on the Colorado River in western Arizona to trade for supplies. In 1862, Abraham H. Peeples prospected for gold and traded with these Indians, trying to find out where their gold nuggets came from. The Indians all said that they could not lead him to the source of the gold, or they would be killed by their tribe.

Peeples finally convinced an Apache Indian to show him one of the gold sites. Peeples was accompanied by Jack Swilling or Joseph Walker (possibly Joe Walker, the famous trapper and mountain man) and two or three other white men who were secretly following from a distance. The Apache failed to show up but was later confronted by Peeples and persuaded to lead him and his friends to the gold site. The party left La Paz and headed northeast toward a mountain range. La Paz was a small mining community where Mexicans had been placer mining. This expedition was also led by Pauline (or Powell) Walker, a famous mixed-blood Cherokee trapper and scout who led the Peeples party up the Hassayampa River.

Before reaching the mountains, the Apache suddenly refused to go any farther. Jack Swilling threatened to kill the Indian guide if he did not continue to lead them to the gold. The Apache pleaded to Major Peeples for protection. The Indian told Peeples that they were very near the gold, which was scattered on the floor of a small canyon. When night came, the Indian disappeared.

The white men continued to the mountains and after two days entered a small gulch with a creek. They followed the creek up to the foot of the highest peak and set up camp. The miners found color in the stream, which they named Weaver Creek. A Mexican herder with the party went up the mountain and found large nuggets of gold on the ground and native gold in the rock. After the herder brought samples of the gold to the camp, the white men hurried to the top of what became Rich Hill, located between Congress Hill and Peeple's Valley. They each quickly gathered $500 to $600 worth of gold, although one story said that Peeples picked up several thousand dollars' worth of gold before breakfast. In less than a year, the site produced $500,000 in gold from a surface area of about an acre. Rich Hill eventually produced millions of dollars' worth of gold.

Major Peeples, however, did not believe that the fantastic find was the mine the Apache had talked about. Some suggested that the big discovery is yet to be made at another, undiscovered site. It could be in Santa Cruz County southeast of Congress Junction near the Hassayampa River.

Marjorie Jackson Robbery Loot

See Maricopa County.

Montezuma Well Treasure

Reportedly gold ore was located near Montezuma's Castle.

Nazi Gold

A legend claimed that Nazis reportedly stashed $300 million near Chloride or between Yuma and Lukesville. See Mohave County.

Prescott Gold Bars

A $75,000 cache of gold bullion was said to be in the Prescott area.

Red Jack Almer Cache

Red Jack Almer reportedly buried $8,000 in gold coins near Prescott.

Sycamore Canyon/San Ignacio Mine/Geronimo's Lost Mine

In the 1700s, a company of Spanish soldiers from the presidio of Altar in Sonora, Mexico, was sent to attack Mojave Apaches in the Verde Valley. In

Lost gold ore was said to be near Montezuma's Well. *New York Public Library.*

a side canyon off Sycamore Canyon, north of Cottonwood near the Verde River, some Spanish soldiers were said to have discovered a rich quartz outcrop full of gold. Six soldiers with two mules and supplies were left to mine the gold. The rest of the company continued its expedition against the Apaches. The six soldiers built a rock shelter under an overhang, dug out the ore and set up a crude arrastra and furnace to smelt gold bars from the ore.

Apaches in the area harassed the Spanish soldiers at the mine but could not chase them away. The six soldiers mined gold through the fall and into the next summer. As they were running out of supplies, the Spanish soldiers decided to return to their post at Altar. The Spaniards loaded the two mules with refined gold bars. Apaches ambushed them when they came out of the side canyon into Sycamore Canyon. Four Spanish soldiers were seriously wounded in the ambush. The Spaniards were unable to get into Sycamore Canyon and returned to their shelter below the overhang, where the four wounded Spaniards died. The remaining two soldiers stored the gold bars in the mine and covered up the mine entrance. In the darkness of night, the surviving two soldiers fled out of the canyon on the two mules. They eventually made their way to the Spanish presidio at Tubac on the Santa Cruz River ten days later.

Spanish King Charles III ordered all Jesuit missions closed and the Jesuits expelled in 1767. The two surviving Spanish soldiers were detailed to Primeria Alta to escort the Jesuits from the area. The soldiers were sent to Guaymas, guarded the Jesuits and then sailed to San Blas. Finally, the two soldiers ended up in Mexico City.

Years later, hunters reported encountering the remains of an old Spanish mining camp and mine in Sycamore Canyon, but they made no attempt to mine for gold due to Indian hostility. In 1853, a prospector, Clifford Haines, who had been to the California gold fields, was chased into Sycamore Canyon by a band of Mojave Indians. Haines found the remains of an old Spanish mining camp, with an arrastra, mining tools and two-wheeled carts. Haines gathered gold ore from the site and fled from Sycamore Canyon. Haines made his way to Tucson. He had a map to the site, but due to the hostile Indians, he never returned to the Sycamore Canyon mine.

New Mexican John T. Squires eventually came into ownership of Haines's map. Squires formed an exploration group, which entered Sycamore Canyon in 1878. They found the mining camp with rotted sacks containing ore as described in the map. The miners worked the old mine through the summer and transported the gold ore to Santa Fe, New Mexico, for smelting. Apaches overran the mining camp, killing almost all of the miners. Squires and several miners went to Tucson and New Mexico. The Apaches destroyed what remained of the mining camp. Squires later died in a saloon fight.

Hostile Apaches, which had been attacking miners and settlers, were forced to move from the area to a reservation about 1886. Some survivors of Squires's mining group returned to the area but were unable to locate the old Spanish mine. In 1896, William O. "Bearhunter" Howard, a Santa Fe Railroad hunter of wild game, stumbled on the old mine. Howard found two hidebound Spanish books that he took to Flagstaff, where they were put on display. He led a prospecting party to look for the mine but was unable to relocate it. Howard spent eight years searching for it and said that he found it again, but he was unable to get anyone else to return to it with him before he passed away. Between 1920 and 1930, Milt Ferrell, Howard's friend, also looked for the lost mine.

In the early 1920s, an Apache named Jim, who worked around Jerome and Clarksdale, sold small bags of gold nuggets from time to time. Some of these gold nuggets were bean sized. Jim said that he found the gold nuggets at a spring in Sycamore Canyon. Cliff Nelson was said to have panned $1,900 worth of gold from an old Spanish arrastra in Sycamore Canyon in 1941.

The mining center of Jerome in 1909. Several lost mines were nearby. *Library of Congress.*

One of the original Spanish soldiers' descendants traveled to Arizona with a map showing the location of the lost mine. The map had been drawn by one of the two surviving soldiers. The descendant had been a Mexican mine supervisor and came to Arizona to find and mine the Lost San Ignacio Mine that his ancestor had worked. The descendant took a job at a copper mine at Jerome but died in a mine explosion. His son Paco inherited the old map and unsuccessfully searched for the mine with his friends for a number of years. Paco was drafted into the U.S. Army during World War II and died in combat in New Guinea. Viviene L. George, who searched for the mine with Paco for three summers during high school, wrote that the map was in ancient Spanish and that the landmarks were named differently than contemporary names.

When looking at the map, the mine was to the left of the rock shelter under the overhang. A *vaso* (adobe smelter) and arrastra were set back from the canyon wall, halfway between the rock shelter and the old mine. The mine was in a short box canyon with a narrow mouth that branched off from Sycamore Canyon at a forty-five-degree angle north by northeast from a quarter-circular curve. The map indicated a dip, which may have been a waterfall or ledge. An old adobe or rock house foundations were visible. A rockslide may have covered a rock wall at the foot of the cliff. A stream of water went under a large boulder near the canyon cliff with the old adobe smelter ruins and arrastra stones near there. Several old graves were nearby and marked by stone piles.

One version of this story has the lost Spanish mine map indicating that the site was in Sycamore Canyon between Perkinsville and Jerome in Yavapai County. Above the mine was an Indian's head–shaped rock, with the mine just below the Indian's nose.

A New York City tenderfoot stumbled across the lost mine as indicated in articles in Jerome's *Verde Copper News* and Flagstaff's *Coconino Sun*. One summer, this young man stayed at the Lolomi Lodge on the west rim where

Oak Creek Canyon and Sycamore Canyon joined. He went out exploring with his camera on his first day there and got lost. A search party was organized when he failed to return to the lodge. Three days later, the young man walked into Perkinsville on the Verde River, which was about thirty miles west of the lodge he started from.

He had spent one night at a rock shelter, which might have been on an Indian site. He had taken photographs of the site. When his film was developed, people who looked at the photos were surprised to see the remains of an old arrastra near the rock shelter he had spent the night at. The locals who saw the film had heard about the lost mine, and some of them went with the tenderfoot several times to try to relocate the sites in the pictures. They failed to find the lost mine, and the tenderfoot returned to his home in New York.

The famous Apache Indian chief Geronimo was captured in 1886 and taken to Fort Sill in present Oklahoma, where he was held by the U.S. Army

Chiricahua Apache prisoners with Chief Geronimo (third from the right in the first row), 1886. *National Archives.*

Sycamore Canyon was Apache Chief Geronimo's hideout and the location of a Spanish lost mine. *National Archives.*

as a prisoner. While in prison, Geronimo was said to have talked to his army guards about a lost mine in Sycamore Canyon the Apaches knew about. Sycamore Canyon had been an Apache hideout from their enemies for many years. Geronimo tried to get three soldiers to let him escape. He claimed that he would show them where the lost mine was located. He indicated that the gold deposit was near the Verde River area near Jerome. The Apaches had used it, but a Spanish expedition later located the gold mine and left some men to mine the gold.

There are at least two Sycamore Canyons in Arizona. See De Espejo's Mine, Coconino County.

Treasure of Zonia

Silver bars, gold bullion, Mexican silver and gold pesos and church treasure were supposed to be hidden near Yava, between Kirkland and Hillside.

Walnut Creek Dam Failure Treasures

On February 22, 1890, $5,000 to $7,500 (now worth more than $580,000) in gold in an iron safe was carried away by a flood when the Walnut Grove Dam failed on the Hassayampa River. The dam was built for hydraulic gold mining and irrigation by the Walnut Grove Storage Company. Alexander Brodie, who later became Arizona's governor, was involved with the design and construction of the dam that failed. Brodie was a former U.S. Army officer and engineer. He had wanted a higher design and construction standards for the dam. The dam was a 110-foot-high earth dam with concrete covering and a small spillway. A two-mile-long lake backed up behind the dam.

When the dam failed after heavy rains, a one-hundred-foot-high wall of water went downstream. The safe in Bob Brown's (or Brow's) Saloon/Store was in Fool's Gulch, a construction camp about fifteen miles below the Walnut Grove Dam. The flood destroyed the small town of Seymour (or Seymore or Sycamore), which had a population of about 200 people. Seymour was founded in 1879 by James Seymour and had a main street with about twenty buildings and a stamp mill. The Conger Store in Seymour had $1,500 hidden by its owner that was also washed away. About 100 to 150 people were killed in the flood. At least 83 bodies were recovered after the flood, with some found many years later. This may be on private land or BLM land.

Yuma County

Blue Mountain Gold

In 1699, Padre Eusebio Kino and Juan Mateo Manje were rumored to have led a party that searched for a Blue Mountain that they had been told was rich in silver ore. An expedition searching for the silver deposit had passed through Arizona the previous year.

Kino and Manje traveled south of the Gila River and journeyed down the eastern side of the Copper Mountains, where they were said to have found slag tailings indicating a nearby mine. Metates on the ground made it appear like Indians had been extracting gold from ore. Indians, knowing of the Spanish thirst for gold and silver, were reported to have hidden the mine.

Chemehuevi Indian Gold Mine

The old chief of the Chemehuevi tribe lived along the Colorado River north of Yuma (then Arizona City). The chief came to Yuma to trade gold for needed supplies and whiskey. The traders and citizens of Yuma plied the old chief with whiskey in an attempt to get him to disclose the location of his gold mine. He would only say that there was much gold at the secret location. The old chief reportedly came to Yuma often to trade gold for supplies until 1863. The chief was supposedly killed by members of his tribe who wanted to keep the location of the gold mine a secret.

Fort Yuma Treasure

Several caches of money obtained by fraud or graft were reportedly hidden in or near old Fort Yuma. Fort Yuma is on the California side of the Colorado River.

Frenchmen's Lost Mine

Three Frenchmen were said to have discovered a fabulous gold mine and brought back $6,000 to $8,000 worth of gold to the Hooper & Company store in Yuma in 1864. The Frenchmen bought supplies from the store and headed east. They reportedly left $8,000 in gold with Hooper & Company for safekeeping. A group of five Mexican miners in Yuma heard about the Frenchmen's find and followed them out of town. The Frenchmen camped at what is thought to be Agua Caliente, a hot spring on the Yuma–Maricopa County line, south of the Eagle Tail Mountains. The next day, the Frenchmen went northward and then reversed direction back to Agua Caliente, where they again set up camp. They split up during the night, each going in a different direction. The Mexican miners knew that they had been discovered and gave up following the Frenchmen.

As a young boy, a Mexican man said that he stayed at the Frenchmen's camp. He discovered that the Frenchmen were burying their gold nuggets in yeast powder tins. He said the camp was located on the west side of the Eagle Tail Mountains near a stream in a mesquite grove. The three Frenchmen never returned to Yuma to get their gold deposited with Hooper & Company.

In 1868, Abraham H. Peeples said that he found three Frenchmen working the placer mine while going through the Harquahala Mountains, north of the Eagle Tails. Later, Peeples reported returning through the same area and finding the camp burned and one human skeleton.

Colonel King S. Woolsey reported in 1873 that he found a pile of rich ore while chasing Apaches through the Eagle Tails. The ore was taken to Yuma, where it was reported to be similar to the gold the three Frenchmen had brought in years before. It was speculated that the three Frenchmen may have abandoned the ore when they were attacked and killed by Indians. This could be in La Paz County.

Grey's Lost Spanish Mine

Before the Yuma Indians' revolt due to being forced by the Spanish out of the area, as the Yumas had been enslaved to work in the Spanish mines, the mine locations were reportedly tribal secrets passed down through generations.

Englishman Reginald Grey came from the California gold fields and married one of the Yuma Indian women. He settled down as a member of the Yuma tribe. When he learned about a hidden Spanish mine, he tried to get his wife to tell him where it was located.

One day, Grey and his Yuma wife traveled through the Adonde Range and camped at Bakers Tank. She told him that they were near an old Spanish mine where the Yumas were once forced by the Spaniards to work. Grey excitedly asked her to show him the mine, but she refused. Finally, she reluctantly agreed to go to the old mine and gather up some of the gold ore. She returned to their camp with a sack of rich gold ore. Upon Grey's urging, she went back to the mine and brought back another sack of rich ore. Grey and his wife returned to their Yuma village, where Grey refined the gold ore to gold.

Grey's wife would later go up into the mountains and return with another sack of gold ore. The Yuma tribe did not like anyone taking gold from the

Many lost treasures and lost mines were associated with Yuma Indians and their uprisings. *Library of Congress.*

hated Spanish mine. Grey's wife disappeared on one of her trips to the mountains. It was likely that the Yumas murdered her for transgressing tribal taboos. The Yumas ordered Grey to leave the area. Fearing that he would be murdered, he fled. The Yumas supposedly hid the Spanish mine entrance. The Adonde Range is between Ligurta and Welton, north of I-17.

Lost Belle McKeever Mine

Near Gila Bend in 1869, Abner McKeever and his daughter, Belle McKeever, were at his placer mine when they were captured by a band of Apaches. Abner was released, but his daughter was not. The Apache band split up when U.S. Army soldiers started tracking them down. The soldiers also split up into small detachments to try to recapture the young girl. One detachment consisted of Sergeant Crossthwaite, Private Joe Wormley and Private Eugene Flannigan. This trio lost the trail of the Apaches they had been following and became lost in the desert and the Granite Wash Mountains. They were without food and water when they stumbled onto a spring. They killed some small animals to eat and refreshed themselves with the water.

They found gold nuggets at the spring and looked for the source of the gold. They found two nearby veins of gold ore. One vein was said to have been sixteen feet wide. It was said they collected about fifty pounds of the rich gold ore and headed for civilization. They struggled south toward the Gila River and ran out of water and food. Crossthwaite and Wormley both fell to the ground, exhausted and dying. Flannigan made it to the Gila River on his hands and knees and was rescued.

A rescue party was formed to search for the other two soldiers. Crossthwaite was dead when he was found, and Wormley was almost dead. Wormley and Flannigan told their rescuers about the gold ore they were carrying but were unsure where their mine was. Flannigan died in 1880 in Phoenix, and Wormley spent the rest of his life searching for the gold veins. Author Harold Bell Wright also searched for this lost mine, which was called the Lost Belle McKeever Mine. Supposedly it was located on the west side of the Granite Mountains.

Lost Bicuner Mine

Said to be in the Laguna Mountains close to Squaw Creek.

Lost Camel's Tank Mine

Prospectors John Gordan and Jan Perea were in the Colorado Desert north of Gila Bend when they ran out of supplies and were low on water. Exhausted and resting beside a boulder, they saw a camel that had escaped from the U.S. Army's camel corps experiment in the distance. Knowing that the camel was heading for water, they followed it to a small tank (depression) containing water. After they satisfied their thirst at the tank, they found gold nuggets there and filled their pockets. They made it safely back to Yuma. Several weeks later, they left Yuma looking for the tank and gold nuggets but never found it.

Lost Canyon of Gold

Said to be in north Yuma County.

Lost Castle Dome Mine

An old Mexican prospector searched the Castle Dome Mountains. He left the Old King of Arizona Mine (Kofa Mine) heading for Ehrenberg. On the way, he found an outcrop of ore and took a sample. Later, while in California, he had the sample assayed and discovered it had a high gold content. Before the prospector could return and mine the gold, he suddenly died. This is supposedly located near the Kofa Mountains near the Colorado River between Ehrenberg and the Old King of Arizona Mine.

Lost Cowboy Gold Mine

A cowboy was said to have found rounded black pebbles in an old canal at the base of a hill in the early 1860s while working on a ranch. An Indian raid on the ranch killed several cowboys, so the ranch was abandoned. The surviving cowboy traveled east and asked a miner what the black pebbles were. The miner told the cowboy that they were hematite. The pebbles were later crushed and found to contain gold. The cowboy eventually returned to the old canal but found no more black pebbles. This is rumored to be along the Colorado River north of Yuma.

Lost Father and Son Mine

Between 1895 and 1900, a prospector went to get his son to help him mine a gold deposit south of Topock on the west side of the Gila Mountains. While en route to get his son, he showed the train conductor at Needles a sack of gold nuggets worth $30,000 and gave the conductor a handful of nuggets. The prospector and his son returned to the mine and were later found dead next to their dead burros in the desert. They were thought to have been murdered by Indians, and their mine was lost.

Lost Gold Stream

A Papago Indian boy was taking an orphan girl from Sonora, Mexico, to Gila City (east of Yuma) when she became dehydrated and could go no farther at the base of a cliff in the Cabeza Prieta Mountains. The boy found a nearby watering hole that was thought to be Tule Well and revived the young girl with water. He also showed her a nearby stream below, which they visited. It had a layer of gold nuggets in it. They took some of them and continued on to Gila City, where she was taken in by his relatives. She later married George Whistler, but he was killed in a fight. She made a deal with Tom Childs to share the gold nuggets if the placer mine were found. Childs looked for it but never found it. It was thought that the stream may have moved and the nuggets were covered up by dirt carried by the rain or blown by the wind.

Lost Indian Mine

Rumored to be in the Adonde Range.

Lost Jabornero (Soapmaker) Mine

See Pima County.

Lost John Nummel's Gold Mine

In the 1920s or 1930s, while on a trip from the Red Cloud Mine to La Fortuna Mine, John Nummel stopped to take a drink from his canteen under a palo verde tree. He saw a ledge of dirty quartz with free gold next to him. He continued on his journey to La Fortuna Mine but was never able to find the site again. He told this tale before he died in 1948 at the Pioneer's Home in Prescott. Writer Harold O. Wright wrote this tale and the one that follows. The trail between the mines went across Yuma Wash some three miles from the Colorado River. This lost mine was said to be near the Colorado River between Yuma Wash and Norton's Landing.

Lost John Nummel's Silver Mine

John Nummel was on a hike from the shut-down Red Cloud Mine (where he was the caretaker) to his cabin located several miles northwest of Norton's Landing on the Colorado River when he picked up some interesting rocks. Nummel was always taking different routes to prospect between these two locations. He added the rocks to his rock collection at his cabin. One day, Yuma miner Walter Riley visited John Nummel and took an interest in one of the rocks in the collection. He asked Nummel if he could assay it. Nummel agreed. It turned out to be very rich silver ore. Nummel couldn't remember where he picked up the rock and was said to have searched for it. One theory was that the rich ore rock came from a mine between the Red Cloud Mine and Mohaves Tanks that was worked by a Dutchman.

Lost Laguna Treasure

A party of miners with reportedly fifty pounds of gold nuggets was attacked and massacred near where the Laguna Dam was later built. Their gold was supposedly buried in a nearby gorge. This could be in California.

Lost Lead Mine

Said to be on the north side of the Harquahala Mountains.

Lost Lord Duppa Mine

See Maricopa County.

Lost Pancho Gold Mine

In the Little Horn Mountains, a Tonto Apache called Pancho told Jose Alvardo about a fabulous gold deposit. Jose Alvardo was the son of former Mexican California Governor Juan Bautista Alvardo. Jose Alvardo owned a ranch where during the Indian Wars about five hundred captured Apaches camped under guard of the U.S. Army before they were marched to the San Carlos Reservation. The Apaches were starving, so Jose Alvardo killed some of his cattle to feed them. Pancho and other Apaches never forgot Jose Alvardo's generosity in those times. Later, Pancho and his family camped on the ranch, and the elderly Pancho came to Jose Alvardo and wanted to guide him to a rich gold deposit to repay his debt of gratitude.

Jose Alvardo and two Mexicans were led by Pancho on trails into the Palomas Mountains and White Tank Mountains on the Kofa-Mohawk Road that led to the King of Arizona (Kofa) Mine. They turned northeast off the road and went through Engesser Pass and camped. Pancho and the two Mexicans got into a heated discussion. An angry Pancho led the party to Alamo Spring the next morning. Pancho left the camp there to go hunting and told them to continue east to an old riverbed with a well. He would catch up with them after hunting. Pancho caught up with them carrying a reddish-black rock that contained gold and silver. That night, Pancho woke Jose Alvardo early in the morning, and the two walked out of the camp a short way to talk. Pancho pointed and told Jose Alvardo that the location of the gold and silver deposit was about 1.5 miles away in a side wash. After the two returned to camp, Pancho left and was never seen again. Jose Alvardo and the two Mexicans returned to his ranch.

Jose Alvardo never returned to find the mine, as he became ill and died. Before dying, Jose Alvardo told his son Jose Alvardo Jr. about the location of the mine. It was several years before his son went to find the mine. Jose

Alvardo Jr. found Alamo Spring but was unable to find the old well and other markers. Supposedly, the lost mine was on the north side of the Little Horn Mountains. This could be in La Paz County.

Lost Quartzsite Mine
This could be near Quartzsite.

Lost Rancho de Las Yumas Mine
Supposedly forty miles north of Yuma on the east side of the Colorado River. See Rood Treasure.

Lost Sapori Mine/Treasure
See Pima County.

Lost Shepherd Girl Mine
May be in southern Yuma County.

Lost Sixshooter Mine No. 1
In Penfield's *A Guide to Treasure in Arizona*, this lost mine is listed as being in Yuma County. See also the Lost Sixshooter Mine No. 1 in La Paz County.

Lost Squawman Gold Mine
Supposedly located near the Bakers Tanks.

Lost Three Dutchman Mine
See Maricopa County.

Lost Trego Mountains Silver Ledge
Eugene L. Conrotto's *Lost Gold and Silver Mines of the Southwest* has this silver ledge in the Trego Mountains lost and found five different times. The first find was by a Mexican who said he got an ore sample less than one day's trip north of the Silver Clip Mine. The prospector gave the ore sample to Jose Maria Mendivil. Mendivil had discovered another ore deposit that became the Silver Clip Mine and sold his claim for only $200. The Silver Clip Mine produced about $1 million in silver from 1883 to 1887.

The Silver Clip Mine's superintendent, Pickenbaugh (nicknamed Pennybacker), was led to a silver ledge north of the Clip Mine by an Indian. Pickenbaugh did not follow up on the silver ledge until after he retired. He and Bert Hart looked for this silver ledge several times but failed to find it.

Santiago Lopez was running cattle up Clip Wash and herded them up a pass north of Clip Mountain. He, too, reportedly found the silver ledge. After going to Yuma, he returned to look for the ledge but never found it again.

Julian Parra was the son of Flisario Parra, who discovered the Mesquite Diggings in California's Chocolate Mountains. Julian Parra reportedly found the silver ledge and even placed a mining claim monument on it but never returned to mine it.

In 1951, Earl Kerr also claimed to have found the silver ledge while on a prospecting trip with George Converse and Ummer Ferrar. He reported to his companions that he found an andesite-red granite contact about four feet high, about thirty feet long and fifteen feet wide. He grabbed a sample before rejoining his friends. Kerr died before he could return to the lost mine. The sample he grabbed did not assay well.

Mission La Purísima Concepción and Mission Bicuner Treasures

A Spanish gold mine was operated near Mission San Pedro y San Pablo de Bicuner in the Laguna Mountains. A Spanish gold placer district known as the Laguna Placers is located east of the Colorado River near Laguna, Arizona, downstream of Imperial Dam. The Mission La Purísima Concepción and Mission San Pedro y San Pablo de Bicuner were established by Padre Francisco Garces and three other padres along with about fifty colonists, workers, soldiers and their families. More Spanish colonists later arrived.

On July 17, 1781, the Yuma Indians revolted against their mistreatment by the Spaniards. The Yumas attacked the two missions and towns in the area, killing almost all the Spaniards, including Franciscan Padre Francisco Garces and three padres, thirty-one soldiers, twenty male settlers, twenty women and twenty children. The Yumas captured sixty-seven women and children. Most of the captured women and children were later rescued and sent back to Sonora.

After sacking the Spanish missions and towns, the Indians were rumored to have transported gold to the base of Picacho Peak (or Squaw Peak or Sugarloaf) in Picacho Peak State Park or threw it into the Colorado River according to Yuma legend.

In the early 1840s, Yuma Indians trading in San Diego created much attention since they spent Spanish coins dated 1776, which they said came from old ruins of the Spanish towns along the Colorado River, where the money had been buried. A group of Anglos and Mexicans went to the old pueblos and looked for buried treasure but failed to find anything. Three

San Diego men—Thomas Russell, Peter Weldon and Francisco Ruiz—were arrested and tried by Mexican authorities for looking for treasure without a license in the Mexican territory in 1836. In 1858, placer gold mines at Laguna and Gila were developed after the Americans took over southern Arizona. They were developed based on tales from the earlier Spanish mines in the area. See Picacho Peak Treasure, Pinal County.

Old Mose's Lost Dutch Oven Mine

This could be in northeastern Yuma County.

Redondo Ruins Treasure

Don Jose Maria Redondo got rich from gold mining and other businesses. He had a large ranch from the public lands he had appropriated. His land was fifteen miles north of Yuma. He had three hundred employees and a two-story adobe headquarters called Hacienda de San Ysidro, which had many outbuildings. He and his brother James owned stores in Yuma. He was in the Arizona territorial legislature and was later Yuma's mayor. The U.S. government divided up his lands, as it claimed he had no title to them. Don Redondo ended up with just one section of land in about 1874. He was rumored to have hidden his treasure at his home, Hacienda de San Ysidro, along the Colorado River.

Rood Treasure

William Rood was said to have cached money (several chests of gold coins) between La Paz and Yuma in 1870 (or 1875) on the Rancho de las Yumas on the east bank of the Colorado River about forty miles north of Yuma. Rood drowned in April 1870 when the boat he and his foreman Pointdexter were riding in hit a snag and capsized while crossing the Colorado River to pay some woodcutters who had done work for Rood. Some suspect that his foreman caused the boat to capsize so he could get Rood's treasure. The foreman and the foreman's wife looked unsuccessfully at the ranch for Rood's cache. The only money found in his estate was a few hundred dollars deposited with Yuma merchants. He was known to have had a lot of hidden gold at his ranch. His two daughters were at a Los Angeles convent when he died. The daughters searched for his lost caches. Several of his caches have reportedly been recovered, including $1,000 in $20 gold coins found in the walls of his rancho in 1897. See Lost Rancho de las Yumas Mine.

Sunlit Cave Treasure

See La Paz County.

Telegraph Pass Lost Treasure

A legend claimed that in 1870, an iron pot containing a $50,000 in gold coins and jewelry was cached south of Goodyear near Telegraph Pass at a campsite with a small butte to east. The cache reportedly was near a level campsite between a low butte on the east side and below Montezuma's Head in the Estrella Mountains.

Wagon Train Massacre Treasure

A wagon train was reportedly attacked and its members massacred at O'Nell Pass. A lost treasure was said to have been associated with this massacre.

Yuma Crossing Treasure

About three miles west of Yuma, the Yuma Crossing on the Colorado River between Arizona and California was a key travel route. On the east bank of the Colorado River, Dr. Able Lincoln established a ferry in the 1850s. Dr. Lincoln was heading home from the Mexican-American War when he heard about the discovery of gold in California while on a ship at the mouth of the Rio Grande off the coast of Texas and Mexico. He left the ship and went on a road that passed through Yuma Crossing on his way to California. Not finding much gold in California, he returned to Yuma Crossing in January 1850 and decided that he could make more money in the ferry business. He was very successful. He wrote to his parents in Illinois reporting that in three months he had made more than $60,000 ferrying thousands of travelers. He had many men working for him.

John Joel Glanton was born in South Carolina and was known as a Texan. Glanton led a gang of Anglo-American outlaws and became Lincoln's partner. Glanton had been in the Texas Cavalry during the Mexican-American War and was arrested for murdering a Mexican during the war. Later, Glanton killed a soldier in San Antonio and fled to Mexico, where he led a gang of Apache scalp hunters who were paid by the Mexican state of Chihuahua for killing Apaches and bringing in their scalps in for bounties. When the scalp hunters ran out of Apaches to kill, the gang killed Mexicans and tried to sell their scalps for bounties. The Mexicans figured this out and put a bounty of $8,000 on Glanton. Glanton and his gang went to Lincoln's Ferry at Yuma in February 1850.

The Yuma Crossing Treasure was cached somewhere in this area along the Colorado River. *Library of Congress.*

Glanton raised the ferry prices from $3 for a man and animal to $10 if they were heading to California. He raised the price to one ounce of gold ($16) if the traveler was coming from California. This ferry had competition downstream at Algodones, Mexico, where Yuma Indians and an Irishman named Callaghan ran that ferry. An emigrant party under Colonel (or General) Anderson (or Patterson) built ferryboats to cross the Colorado River after refusing to pay Glanton and Lincoln to use their ferryboats. The emigrant party gave the boats to the Yumas, who charged $1 per person, $1 per pack and $1 per horse to cross the Colorado River. Glanton and his men decided to get rid of their cheaper charging competition. Callaghan was murdered, and the ferryboat was cut loose and floated downstream. Glanton also reportedly killed a man from Tennessee and took $1,200 from him.

A group of Yumas met with Glanton and his men, as they were sure that Callaghan had been murdered by Glanton and his gang. Glanton was confrontational and hit Yuma Chief Caballo en Pelo with a club and kicked him. Glanton threatened to kill an Indian for every Mexican the Yumas ferried across the Colorado River.

Glanton and his gang went to San Diego for supplies and amusement. When Glanton and his gang returned to Yuma Crossing, the Yumas attacked Glanton, his gang, Able Lincoln and the workers at the ferry at night. Glanton, Dr. Lincoln and most of the gang and ferry workers were massacred. Several Mexicans were part of this plot, as Glanton's gang had reportedly kidnapped their wives.

Three men who worked for Glanton and Lincoln escaped. They went to Los Angeles and made a deposition to Alcalde Don Abel Stevens about the massacre. William Carr reported that Able Lincoln had $50,000 in silver and between $20,000 and $30,000 (at about $16 to $17 per ounce then) in gold. Glanton was supposed to have cached his share of the ferry fees, which may have been about $80,000.

Jeremiah Hill later reported that he learned from an Indian that the Yumas had found three bags of silver three feet high and two feet wide and a bag of gold one foot high and a foot thick that belonged to Dr. Able Lincoln. The Yumas distributed this money throughout their tribe.

Emigrants passing through the area after the massacre reportedly sold the Yumas clothes and other items for $13,000. Glanton may have buried his treasure along the Colorado River near his ferry or among the outbuildings used by the ferry. There is one story told by an old Yuma who claimed that Glanton's treasure was found by the Yumas and thrown into the Colorado River.

Yuma Indians retaliated against the Glanton Gang by murdering John Glanton, Able Lincoln and most of the ferrymen. *Library of Congress.*

The new state of California (created in 1850) panicked over the Yuma Indian uprising and sent the Gila Expedition to punish the Indians and recover the treasure. Members of the expedition were said to have robbed Mexicans returning from the California gold fields at Yuma. The expedition was a fiasco and cost California $113,487.25 after four years.

Gold coins from 1850 or earlier would be worth a fortune, especially if there were rare gold coins in the cache. Glanton's cache would be worth millions of dollars today.

MINING

Arizona is a producer of many minerals, mostly copper, gold, silver, lead, zinc, manganese, iron, tungsten, uranium and mercury. Early Arizona mines were mostly placer gold mines. Lode mines usually required smelting and were expensive to mine due to transportation distances of the ore, which sometimes had to be transported out of Arizona for crushing and treatment.

Arizona has produced more than 16 million ounces of gold. Yavapai County is the number one gold producer, and Mohave County is number two. Ten Arizona counties contain forty-two gold mining districts. Most lost gold mines are associated with these gold mining districts. Currently, gold production is mostly a byproduct of Arizona's copper mines.

In 1774, Spanish priest Manuel Lopez had Papago Indians washing placer gold on the slopes of Quijotoa Mountains in Pima County. Early Spanish and Mexican gold mining was done in the Oro Blanco District in Santa Cruz County and the Arivaca District in Pima County. During the California Gold Rush, the gold seekers heard stories of prior Spanish and Mexican gold and silver mining in Arizona Territory. After the easy placer gold was mined out in California, some of these miners went to search for gold and silver in Arizona Territory.

In 1855, U.S. Army Lieutenant Sylvester Mowry was stationed at Fort Yuma when he found silver ore on the south side of the Santa Rita Mountains about twelve miles south of present Patagonia. Mowry became a politician and mining entrepreneur who ran afoul of the Union army during the Civil War and had issues over his Southern sentiments.

A large Arizona mine complex. *Library of Congress.*

In 1862, placer mining began in the Bradshaw Mountains after Joseph "Joe" Walker led a group of Californians into Arizona to look for gold. Unlike most of California, water for placer mining was scarce and harder to secure.

The Vulture Mine was discovered by Austrian Henry Wickenburg in 1863 or 1864. The mine was a complex of shale, andesite, granite, porphyry and quartz. The Vulture Mine's gold-bearing quartz veins resulted in the most productive mine in Arizona and has produced 340,000 ounces of gold and 260,000 ounces of silver.

During the Civil War, Union California Volunteer Captain John Moss was stationed at Fort Mohave. Moss found a deposit of gold in the Black Mountains that he and his men mined. They reportedly recovered $240,000 in ore from the Moss Mine.

In 1877, prospector Ed Schieffelin, who was operating out of the U.S. Army post of Camp Huachuca, was told that the only thing he was going to find looking for gold and silver was his tombstone. Schieffelin had a sense of humor and named his tremendous strike in Cochise County Tombstone in 1877.

Apache County has microscopic gold in clays in the Triassic formation in its desert areas. Gold and silver has been found along with copper in the southern part of Apache County. Some small placer gold deposits also have been reported. There are seven lost mine stories from Apache County in this book.

Cochise County has produced more than 2.7 million ounces of gold mined from 1879 to 1959. More than half of this total came as a byproduct of copper mining in deposits near Bisbee. Very little placer gold was mined in this county. About 5.8 million ounces of silver were produced by the Tombstone mines in one year. Tombstone was a large porphyry dike with faults and joints that contained lots of minerals. There are nine lost mine stories from Cochise County in this book.

Coconino County has microscopic gold in clays in the Triassic formation in its desert. There are twelve lost mine stories from Coconino County in this book.

Gila County produced 240,500 ounces of gold through 1959, with two-thirds of that total coming as a copper byproduct. There are ten lost mine stories from Gila County in this book.

Graham County produced some gold from quartz outcrops and other lode deposits. The Clifton Copper District is in Graham County. There are three lost mine stories from Graham County in this book.

Greenlee County produced both placer gold and lode gold. Some gold was also produced as a byproduct of silver and copper mine production. There are two lost mine stories in Greenlee County in this book.

La Paz County has eight lost mine stories in this book.

Maricopa County, the home of the Lost Dutchman Mine story, produced more than 428,000 ounces of gold. Most of this gold production was from the Vulture Mine. Silver, copper, lead and zinc ores are in Paleozoic and Archean rock generally in metamorphosed contacts and granite. There was a small amount of gold from placer deposits. There are twenty-six lost mine stories from Maricopa County in this book.

This dry wash design captured placer gold in Arizona desert areas. *New York Public Library.*

Gold and silver were byproducts of this now abandoned copper mine at Bisbee. *New York Public Library.*

Mohave County produced more than 2.4 million ounces of gold through 1959. Most of the gold came from the San Francisco Mining District near Oatman as lode gold. Silver has been found in sulphides or selenides and other varieties in granite. There are also placer gold deposits in this county. There are five lost mine stories from Mohave County in this book.

Navajo County has microscopic gold in clays in the Triassic formation in its desert areas. There are five lost mine stories from Navajo County in this book.

Pima County made more than $3.2 million worth of gold through 1931. Two-thirds of this was a byproduct of copper mining. Ajo has a huge open pit copper mine. More than 990,000 ounces of gold were produced as a copper byproduct from 1924 to 1959. The Arivaca area has placer deposits and lode deposits, with mining from the Spanish period. There are twenty-five lost mine stories from Pima County in this book.

Pinal County produced 893,350 ounces of gold from 1858 to 1959. Gold is produced from both lode and placer mines in Pinal County. Silver, lead, manganese, barite and copper ores are found in a variety of granite, limestone, sandstone, quartz and diorite rocks. There are six lost mine stories from Pinal County in this book.

Santa Cruz County has had gold production since the Spanish period, with more than 100,200 ounces of gold documented as having been produced. There are ten lost mine stories from Santa Cruz County in this book.

Yavapai County had its first lode gold mined in 1863. It is reported as producing about 3.5 million ounces of lode gold and 266,804 ounces of placer gold through 1959. Gold and silver ore are in metamorphic andesite, often in quartz veins. Yavapai County has been the number one gold producing county in Arizona. The Jerome area has produced more than 1.5 million ounces of gold. There are fifteen lost mine stories from Yavapai County in this book.

Yuma County has nine mining districts that as a total produced more than 771,000 ounces of gold, but most of the other mining districts had under 10,000 ounces of gold mined in each district. Silver and lead ores are found in metamorphic rocks and granite in quartz veins. There are twenty-seven lost mine stories from Yuma County in this book.

AZTEC AND INDIAN LOST TREASURE AND LOST MINES

In 1519, Hernando Cortez and his small army of Spaniards landed on the east coast of Mexico and found some Indians wearing gold jewelry. The Spaniards had just overcome the Muslim Moors in Spain and were full of religious zeal and the desire to obtain wealth and power for Spain and themselves. Cortez and his small Spanish army were joined by a large army of Indian allies who wished to overthrow the Aztec empire, which had kept them in virtual slavery and sacrificed many of their tribesmen to Aztec gods.

Cortez's army marched inland, fighting many battles before entering the Aztec capital of Tenochtitlan (now Mexico City) in 1520. By a ruse, they captured Aztec emperor Montezuma and collected vast amounts of gold, silver and jewels. Behind a plastered-over door in Montezuma's palace, Cortez and his men found a large hall full of treasure that included gold and silver bars and ore, jewelry and other valuable objects. One of the Spaniards, Bernal Diaz, wrote, "It seemed to me as if all the riches in the world were in that room."

Cortez had to take part of his army back to the eastern Mexican coast to meet another Spanish army under Pánfilo de Narváez, who had been sent by the Cuban Governor Don Diego Velasquez to take over what Cortez had conquered. Cortez and Velasquez had a violent disagreement over who was in charge of the new lands. While Cortez decisively defeated Narváez's forces, the Aztecs attacked the Spanish forces in Tenochtitlan and drove

Montezuma and Cortez met in Mexico City. The resulting war caused the Aztecs to hide much of their gold and treasure. *Library of Congress.*

them out of the city. Cortez was reinforced by the survivors of Narváez's army and finally conquered the Aztec empire by recapturing Tenochtitlan in 1521 after many vicious battles that killed hundreds of thousands. Cortez and the conquering Spaniards sent vast quantities of gold, silver and jewels back to Spain. Large numbers of Spaniards and Europeans then traveled to the New World in search of fortune and fame.

A number of legends sprang up about the Aztecs and other Indian tribes hiding treasure from the Spaniards in what are now the states of Arizona, California, Colorado, New Mexico and Utah in the western United States in addition to places in Mexico and Central America.

One account noted that in 1520, after the Spaniards had been driven out of Tenochtitlan, the Aztecs gathered vast quantities of gold, silver and jewels to move their treasures out of the reach of the Spaniards. Seven caravans of one hundred men, with each man carrying sixty pounds of treasure, were said to have traveled north and then west into the mountains to hide the treasure. This area may have been northern Mexico or possibly the Four Corners area of Arizona, Colorado, New Mexico and Utah. Montezuma's Aztec treasures were said to be hidden in Coconino, La Paz, Mohave and Pinal Counties.

The Arizona Indians are said to have had many lost mines. Many Indians found gold and silver deposits in their travels over the years. The Spaniards, Mexicans and Americans often took over these mines. Some of the mines became lost when the Indians ran the miners off from what had been their mine.

Geronimo and his lost mine are a prominent theme in several lost treasure tales. See Geronimo's Lost Gold Mine, Cochise County and Sycamore Canyon Mine/San Ignacio Mine/Geronimo's Lost Mine, Yavapai County.

LOST SPANISH TREASURE AND LOST MINES

Many lost treasure and lost mine tales come from the Spanish period of Arizona occupation. In 1583, a Spanish expedition marched west from Santa Fe under New Mexican Governor Don Antonio de Espejo into present Arizona. De Espejo was a mining engineer trained in Córdoba, Spain, who was wealthy from his Mexican mining ventures. The expedition traveled up the Rio Grande to the Rocky Mountains and into the Colorado Plateau. The Espejo Expedition found huge copper deposits near present Jerome, close to Mingus Mountain, but reportedly no silver or gold mines. It turned out that much gold and silver were also in the copper deposits.

The northern frontier of New Spain was the home of many Indians who continually resisted Spanish settlements and exploration. The Indians were often at war with one another also. They were scattered in small tribes and villages. Due to the Spanish need for labor, slavery continued along the frontier, which caused many Indian uprisings.

Padre Juan de la Assumpcion traveled northward into Sonora and maybe southern Arizona in 1538. In July 1539, Francisco de Ulloa sailed from the Gulf of California (Sea of Cortez) to the Colorado River Delta and the mouth of the mighty Colorado River.

New Mexico became a royal Spanish colony in 1609. Pedro de Peralta became New Mexican governor on March 30, 1609, and proceeded to stabilize the situation between Indians and colonists. Soldiers under his rule were more interested in finding gold and silver than enslaving Indians. Peralta and his descendants are associated with many lost mine and treasure stories, including the Lost Dutchman Mine. In 1610, Don Pedro de Peralta led an expedition from New Spain that founded La Villa Real de la Santa Fe de San Francisco de Assisi or Santa Fe (Holy Faith), New Mexico, located about thirty miles south of the old capital of San Gabriel. Peralta made Santa Fe the new capital of New Mexico, which included Arizona. By 1630, the population of Santa Fe was about 250. From Santa Fe, about 250 Franciscan padres were sent to spread Christianity to New Mexico and parts of eastern Arizona. These padres established many missions.

Although slavery was illegal, many Indians were treated as slaves in the Spanish frontier areas. Spanish governors often started wars with peaceful tribes so they could enslave the Indians and sell them to mines and ranches in Mexico. The Spanish extracted tribute in the form of corn and clothing from Indians. Slave raiding expeditions by tribes friendly to the Spanish, as well as by Spanish settlers, were common in Spanish colonial times.

In 1592, Spain made it illegal for priests to own and run mines and strengthened that law in 1621 due to the Jesuits trying to circumvent the law. The Jesuits were said to have resisted paying the Royal Fifth to the Spanish Crown. In 1600, much silver was found by Spanish explorers and prospectors in Chihuahua and later in Sonora, Mexico, which then was the northern settled Spanish frontier. Zacatecas, Aguas Calientes, San Luis Potosi, Guanajuato, San Miguel de Allende and Queretaro became great mining districts in Spanish New Spain. Many fortunes were made from the mines south of Arizona, which spurred further exploration and settlement along the northern New Spain frontier. By the early 1660s, the Spanish had mines in a Hopi area in New Mexico called Sierra Azul.

A mining expedition under Captain Marcos Farfan de los Godso consisted of eight soldiers who went to investigate stories of mines near present Jerome. They found rich mineral deposits, probably the same mineral deposits found by Espejo in 1583. Some of those soldiers had been with Espejo in his earlier expedition. An old shaft and large ore dump were found at one mine site. Several wide veins with blue, green, black and white ore were found in the area. Cruzado Indians in the area used the ores to stain their bodies and to color pots and clothing. Samples of the ores were taken back to Onate and the main Spanish party and assayed. One sample was reported to have had eleven ounces of silver per quintal.

A number of Indian revolts interfered with Spanish mining efforts on the northern Spanish frontier. About one thousand Pueblo Indians were killed during the 1598 revolt in New Mexico. Several other revolts in 1599 resulted in about one thousand additional Pueblo Indian deaths. In the fall of 1598, Governor Onate sent a captain to check on salt deposits and silver deposits that Hopi Indians had related to the Spanish. They searched for gold and silver deposits but reportedly found poor assays of the mineral deposits. In late 1603 or early 1604, Captain Geronimo Marquez led a party to or near present Jerome but reported ore veins in New Mexico with little economic value to the Spanish. Onate resigned as the New Mexican governor on August 24, 1607, after being recalled to Spain. Onate was tried and convicted of various crimes relating to his actions against Indians and Spanish colonists in New Mexico and part of Arizona. Onate and his backers had spent 600,000 pesos on the expedition to colonize New Mexico and had no tangible treasure to show for their great expense.

Padre Eusebio Francisco Kino came to Sonora in 1687 and used Mission Nuestra Sonora de los Dolores as his base from which he helped establish missions in present southern Arizona south of the Gila River. Mineral deposits were found in these areas.

In 1691, Jesuits traveled to a Papago (Tohono O'odham) village in Arizona. In 1700, they began construction on Mission San Jose de Tumacacori among the Indians at that village. In 1700, Jesuits built Mission San Xavier del Bac at a Pima Indian village just south of present Tucson. Padre Eusebio Kino wrote, "Many good mines of gold and silver…many rich veins now being established" in his accounts of Primeria Alta, which probably included southern Arizona.

The Hopis had the Sierra Azul Mines, Los Ceros Colorados in Mogui, which were occupied by Apaches. The Spanish wanted to chase the Apaches away to get the amalgam (almagre) or vermillion, which was mercury ore mined in the Zero Colorado. One deposit was thought to have been north of present Williams, Arizona, at Ned Butte. In late 1693, the New Mexican governor, Diego de Vargas, searched for these deposits but did not find them.

There was a Pima Indian revolt in 1695. See Mission Guevavi Treasure and Lost Mine, Santa Cruz County.

Padre Kino died in 1711, and the Spanish missions' influence among Indians declined for several decades. The Spanish pitted Indian tribes against one another along their frontier to serve as a buffer zone. The Pimas served as barriers to Apache raids into Spanish settlements in northern Mexico. The Spanish system had a divide-and-conquer strategy that usually worked on New Spain's northern frontier.

In 1723, there was a Papago and Pima Indian revolt against the Spaniards. See Lost Esmeralda (Emerald) Mine/La Esmeralda Church Treasure, Pima County.

Several treasures are associated with Mission San Xavier del Bac. *John and Bev Passarello.*

In the 1730s, there was a mining rush to Arizonac (modern Arizona and Sonora) and an increase in the number of Jesuits trying to Christianize Indians in what is now southern Arizona. A significant silver discovery occurred in Sonora in 1736 with hundreds of prospectors and miners flooding into the region. Balls of silver up to 300 pounds were discovered. A silver nugget as large as 3,600 pounds was recovered in a mining camp called Arizona, which is Basque for the "good oak tree."

There was some controversy over whether each new silver discovery was a treasure-trove or a silver vein. The Spanish Crown did not want to call the silver discovery area a mining district subject to the Crown's royalty of quinto, but rather wanted all of the silver to belong to the king as a treasure-trove. This caused much controversy between the miners and the king's agents. This was why many mines were not well documented since they were not paying the Crown what the king's agents wanted. Two silver lodes were discovered in about 1750 in the Santa Rita Mountains near Mission San Xavier del Bac, not far from Tucson.

During the Prima Alta Pima Indian revolt on November 20, 1751, a number of hostile Indians attacked and destroyed Mission San Xavier del Bac and Mission San Gabriel de Guevavi, but the mission priests escaped harm. More than one hundred Spaniards were massacred, including many miners. Several lost Spanish mines date from this revolt. See Lost Black Princess Mine/Lost Blonde Mayo Mine, Pima County; Mission San Marcelo Treasure/Sonoyta Mine, Pima County; and Treasure and Lost Mine, Santa Cruz County.

In Santa Cruz County in 1753, Spain built a presidio at Tubac called San Ignacio de Tubac as a result of the Pima Indian Revolt in 1751. Fifty Spanish soldiers were stationed at Tubac, which was the first permanent European settlement in present Arizona besides the missions. Tubac was built to guard the surrounding Spanish gold and silver mines. In 1757, Padre Bernardo Middendorff of the Jesuits founded Mission San Augustine del Tucson.

In 1767, King Charles III expelled the Jesuits from the Spanish lands and from Spain's lands in the Americas. King Charles III had tired of the Jesuit intrigues whose self-interest and plans often conflicted with the king's plans. His plan was similar to what France did to the Knights Templar in 1307. Secret orders from King Charles III were opened on June 24, 1767, in Mexico City, New Spain. Every Jesuit was seized and was to be taken to Vera Cruz for expulsion. On immediate sentence of death, no one was to talk to the Jesuits or give them advance warning regarding their expulsion. In secret, 3,000 Spanish troops surrounded five Jesuit residences and rousted 178 Jesuits from their sleep at 4:00 a.m. in Mexico City. See Lost Esmeralda (Emerald) Mine/La Esmeralda Church Treasure, Pima County; Lost San Pedro Mine/La Mina del San Pedro, Santa Cruz County; Lost Planchas de Plata Mine, Santa Cruz County; and Lost Virgin de Guadalupe Silver Mine/Treasure, Santa Cruz County.

The Primeria Alta Revolt in 1772 resulted in many ranches and villages burned by Indians. See Lost Spanish Silver Mine, Santa Cruz County, and Valverdes Gold, Santa Cruz County.

During the Primeria Alta Revolt of 1772, Arizona missions and ranches were burned. Tubac was abandoned in late 1775 or 1776, with the garrison removed to Tucson. Spanish soldiers later rebuilt the Tubac fort to protect the valuable mines in the area. The commander of Tubac, Juan Bautista de Anza, established a road to San Francisco, California, which he founded in 1776. In 1787, Pima Indian soldiers under Spanish officers returned to garrison Tubac.

In the 1780s, the Spanish had a "Peace by Deceit" doctrine with the Apaches. This plan included giving Indians food, guns and liquor, which gave them some peaceful periods during which mining occurred. Spanish prospectors and miners looked for and developed some Arizona mines.

Spain established two pueblos on the Colorado River on the trail between Mission San Diego de Alcala, California, and Tucson, Arizona. The Spanish pueblos were on the west side of the Colorado River in present California at the upper end of navigation on the Colorado River. The Spanish pueblos were on lands owned by the Yuma Indians. La Purísima Concepción was a pueblo along with a mission established in 1780 at what is now Fort Yuma Hill. This where the Gila River met the Colorado River. In 1851, the ruined site on Fort Yuma Hill was described as consisting of eight to ten adobe structures on about one acre of land.

The pueblo of San Pedro y San Pablo de Bicuner was established in January 1781 in the hills near a Colorado River overflow channel about four or five leagues (eight miles) upstream of La Purísima Concepción at another Yuma village or ranchería. About 160 Spanish, part-Spanish and civilized Indians settled in the two towns. The settlers were generally poor and uneducated and were looking to improve their position. The Yuma Indians who lived along the Colorado River welcomed the newcomers at first, but as the Spanish settlers took the Yuma Indians' food, supplies and land, Yuma resentment arose. Some Yuma Indians were forced to mine for placer and lode gold deposits in the Potholes, Piacho and Cargo Muchacho-Tumco mining districts in California and in the Laguna Mountains of Arizona. Harsh treatment and crimes against the Yuma Indians caused them to rebel.

An organized simultaneous attack by Yuma and some Mohave Indians took place on July 17, 1781, as Spanish settlers were leaving church services in La Purísima Concepción and San Pedro y San Pablo de Bicuner. At La Purísima Concepción, eleven soldiers were killed, while at San Pedro y San Pablo de Bicuner seventeen men and Padre Diaz were killed. San Pedro y San Pablo de Bicuner's church and the town were looted and set afire.

Across the Colorado River on the Arizona side, a detachment of eleven Spanish soldiers under Captain Fernando Rivera y Moncada made a makeshift barricade, which was overrun on July 17 or July 18, 1781, by the Indians. The Spanish soldiers were all killed. Concepción was looted and burned on July 18. On July 19, the Indians killed two captured Franciscan padres, Francisco Garces and Juan Barreneche, with clubs. Church images were destroyed or thrown away, and livestock and horses were taken by the Indians. Several detachments of soldiers in the area were also surrounded and killed. Spanish losses were fifty-five men killed (four Franciscan padres, thirty-one soldiers and twenty settlers), along with twenty women and twenty children killed. Another seventy-six Spaniards (five soldiers, four settlers and sixty-seven women and children) were taken prisoner.

A Spanish expedition led by Lieutenant Colonel Pedro Fages with 110 Spanish soldiers from Tucson and 96 Ootyam Indian allies arrived at the Colorado River in the fall of 1781 along with 600 Indian allies (Halchichoma, Cocomericopa and Gila River Indians). Prisoners held by the revolting Indians were traded for Spanish goods; 5 soldiers and 69 survivors from the attacks by the Yumas and Mohaves were safely recovered. Several battles also took place between the Spanish and their Spanish-allied Indians against the rebelling Indians. The rebellious tribes finally took to the hills and hid. The Spanish expedition returned to Tucson and other settlements, leaving the Colorado River area without any Spanish towns or presidios. Many stories of lost mines and lost treasures come from this period. See Sunlit Cave Treasure, La Plaz County; Picacho Peak Treasure, Pinal County; Lost Ajo Treasure/Lost Carretta (Careta) Canyon and Treasure, Santa Cruz County; and Mission La Purísima Concepción and Mission Bicuner Treasures, Yuma County.

LOST MEXICAN AND AMERICAN MINES

When Mexico revolted against Spain and became an independent country, Arizona and other areas on Mexico's northern frontier became unstable as Indians increased their raids and attempted to drive Mexican settlers out. The new nation of Mexico did not seem to have encouraged mining in the frontier area we call Arizona. Corruption and conflict discouraged open mining along the Mexican frontier. Mexican prospectors and miners seem to have mostly secretly mined gold and silver in the frontier areas and then transported them back to their home regions in Mexico.

Don Ignacio Zuniga, a commander of forts in northern Sonora, wrote that between 1820 and 1835, Apache Indians killed at least five thousand settlers, and about four thousand settlers fled from their ranches and towns. Along the Sonora frontier, only Tubac and Tucson remained in Mexican hands in what is now Arizona. Indians forced many Mexican settlers to withdraw southward or to face death if they remained. Tubac was finally abandoned in 1830 due to Apache Indian attacks but was resettled later. A number of lost mine stories come from this period in Arizona, especially in present Pima County and Santa Cruz County.

In 1835, the frontier Mexican states placed bounties on Apache scalps as a means to eradicate raiding Apaches. In 1837, Chihuahua offered one hundred pesos for each male Apache scalp, fifty pesos for each female Apache scalp and twenty-five pesos for each Apache child scalp.

In Arizona, the rich Santa Rita Copper mines, which had been mined by the Spanish and Mexicans since 1804, were abandoned in 1838 due to

Apache raids. Mangas Coloradas (Red Sleeves) was a Mimbres Apache chief who depopulated many Arizona frontier areas due to his raids. See Lost Peralta Mine, Maricopa County.

Northern and Central Arizona was ceded to the United States as part of the settlement of the Mexican-American War in 1848 under the Treaty of Guadalupe Hidalgo. American and foreign immigrants journeyed through what was then Mexico and what is now southern Arizona, bound for the California gold fields. These travelers reported that whole towns and all the ranches had been abandoned years earlier due to the Apache Indian raids. The travelers wrote that there were rich gold and silver mines in the area, but the Indian attacks had closed down the mines and chased off the miners.

When the easily mined gold in California was depleted, some miners and prospectors left for Arizona. These immigrants had heard tales of abandoned and lost gold and silver mines in Arizona. Some had seen indications of rich minerals in this state when they traveled through on their way to California. See Lost Adams Diggings, Graham County and Maricopa County; Lost Sixshooter Mine No. 1 and Lost Sixshooter Mine No. 2, La Paz County; and Lost Dutchman Mine, Maricopa County.

In 1854, southern Arizona became part of the United States due to the Gadson Purchase, which was negotiated when Mexico and its president, Santa Anna, were in desperate need of cash. The United States paid $10 million for about 27,305 square miles. The United States needed a quicker southern route to California and planned to build a railroad on this route. During treaty negotiations for the Gadsden Purchase, American investors and entrepreneurs began scouting for mining lands to develop in the region.

The establishment of U.S. Army forts and camps throughout Arizona Territory led to many soldiers prospecting and mining gold and silver while off duty and finding gold and silver deposits while they were on patrol and hunting hostile Indians. Many gold and silver deposits were found by soldiers. After leaving the army, many ex-soldiers became prospectors and miners. A number of lost mine stories came from the soldiers and ex-soldiers prospecting efforts. See Lost Soldier Mine, Gila County; Lost Two Soldiers Mine, Maricopa County; Lost Dr. Thorne Mine, Maricopa County; Lost Monument Valley Mine/Lost Pish-la-ki Mine, Navajo County; Heintzelman Mine High Grade Treasure, Pima County; Lost Baboquivari Mountains Mine, Pima County; Lost Two Ex-Soldiers Mine, Pinal County; Yuma's Lost Mine, Pinal County; and Lost Belle McKeever Mine, Yuma County.

Fort Yuma guarded the Yuma Colorado River crossing and kept a watch on the Yuma Indians. *Library of Congress.*

Hostile Indians and the Indian wars prevented settlement and mining in many areas of Arizona Territory. Many prospectors and miners were attacked and killed by the hostile Indians. Miners were forced to abandon their mines and claims for many years. Many lost mine stories come from this period of turmoil, which lasted until about 1890.

OUTLAWS AND THEIR LOOT

Outlaws and outlaw gangs ranged over much of Arizona over the years. They robbed smugglers, pack trains carrying gold and silver, trains and stagecoaches, as well as travelers. Information on outlaws is often sketchy and confusing, as they generally lied about what their real names were, what robberies they committed and who they murdered. The friends and families of outlaws also lied and misled the law enforcement who were looking for outlaws.

Since there were many Arizona gold and silver mines, there were many coins and ingots being transported by mule trains, stagecoaches and trains throughout Arizona. These were tempting targets for outlaws. Arizona has a long border with Mexico, so it was subject to raids from across the border by Mexican outlaw gangs. Mexico was also raided by Anglo-American outlaw gangs. Like today, smuggling often occurred on both sides of the border.

The most infamous Arizona outlaw gang were known as the Cowboys. They rustled cattle in Mexico and Arizona Territory. The Cowboys Gang robbed trains, banks, stagecoaches and mining mills. The Cowboys Gang were a loose band of cowboys turned outlaws that terrorized Arizona Territory for many years. Skeleton Canyon was the site of one of the biggest robberies by the Cowboys Gang. The robbery in July 1881 and treasure associated with the robbery are detailed in Skeleton Canyon Treasure, Cochise County.

The Clantons had a cattle ranch near Charleston, and the McLarys also had a ranch in the area. Both ranches were used by the Cowboys Gang to give legitimacy to the stolen cattle. The stolen cattle seem to have been often sold to feed hungry miners in Tombstone.

The famous shootout at the O.K. Corral in Tombstone occurred on October 26, 1881. "Old Man" Ike Clanton, Billy Clanton, Tom McLary, Frank McLary and Billy Claiborne of the Cowboys Gang were armed and in Tombstone. Lawmen Temporary Assistant Marshal Wyatt Earp, Temporary Assistant Marshal Morgan Earp, Deputy U.S. Marshal and Tombstone Marshal Virgil Earp and Temporary Assistant Marshal Doc Holliday attempted to disarm the five members of the Cowboys. At close range in less than a minute, Billy Clanton, Tom McLary and Frank McLary were killed. Morgan Earp, Virgil Earp and Holliday were wounded.

The surviving members of the Cowboys Gang ambushed and wounded Virgil Earp on December 28, 1881, when he was hit by three shotgun blasts from behind. The Cowboys Gang ambushed Morgan Earp and killed him on March 18, 1882, by firing through a door window while he was playing pool.

Members of the Cowboys Gang generally met violent deaths. The Earps and their lawmen friends killed several of them. Outlaw Johnny Ringo supposedly committed suicide.

A number of lost loot stories were associated with members of the Cowboys Gang. See Charleston Caches, Cochise County; Skeleton Canyon Treasure, Cochise County; and Zwing Hunt Treasure, Cochise County.

Lost train robbery loot includes Alvord-Stiles Gang Loot, Cochise County; Train Robbery Coins, Cochise County; Brown's Outlaw Cache, Coconino County; Roy Gardner's Treasure, Coconino County; and Colossal Cave Bandit Loot, Pima County.

Lost stagecoach robbery loot includes Wells Fargo Loot, Cochise County; Pene Springs Treasure, Coconino County; and Lost Stagecoach Bullion, Mohave County.

Outlaw gangs were present in many areas of frontier Arizona over the years. When Arizona became a state in 1912, it was the last frontier area in the contiguous United States. Arizona outlaw movies include *Tombstone*, *The Town Too Tough to Die*, *Gunfight in the O.K. Corral* and *Wyatt Earp*.

More modern loot is likely hidden in Arizona. The most famous loot in modern times is from the Marjorie Jackson robbery and murder in 1977. See Marjorie Jackson Robbery Loot, Maricopa County.

BIBLIOGRAPHY

Books

Childress, David Hatcher. *Lost Cities and Ancient Mysteries of the Southwest.* Adventures Unlimited Press, 2009.

Clark, Howard D. *Lost Mines of the Old West.* Ghost Town Press, 1946.

Clark, William B. *Gold Districts of California.* Bulletin 193, California Division of Mining and Geology, Sacramento, 1980.

Conrotto, Eugene L. *Lost Gold and Silver Mines of the Southwest.* Dover Publications Inc., 1991.

Dobie, J. Frank. *Apache Gold and Yaqui Silver.* Ballantine Books, 1974.

Drago, Harry Sinclair. *Lost Bonanzas.* Pocket Books, 1967.

Ely, Sims. *The Lost Dutchman Mine—The Fabulous Story of the Seven-Decade Search for the Hidden Treasure in the Superstition Mountains of Arizona.* William Morris and Company, 1953.

Forbes, Jack D. *Apache, Navajo and Spaniard.* University of Oklahoma Press, 1979.

———. *Warriors of the Colorado: The Yumas of the Quechan Nation and Their Neighbors.* University of Oklahoma Press, 1965.

Gaines, W. Craig. *Civil War Gold and Other Lost Treasure.* Rev. ed. Amazon, 2020.

———. *Hispanic Treasure of the Western United States.* Amazon, 2020.

———. *Lost California Treasure.* The History Press, 2023.

Garate, Donald T. *Arizona (Never Arizonac).* Tumacacori National Park, 2006.

Getler, Warren, and Bob Brewer. *Rebel Gold: One Man's Quest to Crack the Code Behind the Secret Treasures of the Confederacy.* Simon & Schuster, 2003.

Gray, Floyd, et al. *Mineral Resources of the Arrastra Mountain/Peoples Canyon Wilderness Study Area, La Paz, Mohave and Yavapai Counties, Arizona.* U.S. Geological Survey Bulletin, 1701. U.S. Government Printing Office, 1989.

Groushko, Michael. *Lost Treasures of the World.* Chartwell Books Inc., 1986.

Haley, James L. *Apaches: A History and Culture Portrait.* University of Oklahoma Press, 1981.

Hart, Herbert M. *Old Forts of the Far West.* Bonanza Books, 1965.

Henson, Michael Paul. *America's Lost Treasures.* Jayco Publishing Company, 1984.

Jameson, W.C. *Buried Treasure of the American Southwest.* August House, 1989.

———. *The Lost Canyon of Gold, Discovering the Lost Adams Diggings.* Two Dot, 2017.

———. *Treasure Hunter: A Memoir of Caches, Curses and Confrontation.* Taylor Trade, 2014.

Kemp, Furman. *The Ore Deposits of the United States and Canada.* Engineering Mining Journal, 1905.

Marx, Robert F. *Buried Treasure of the United States: How and Where to Locate Hidden Wealth.* Bonanza Books, 1978.

Mitchell, John D. *Lost Mines & Buried Treasures Along the Old Frontier.* Rio Grande Press Inc., 1970.

———. *Lost Mines of the Great Southwest.* Rio Grande Press Inc., 1984.

Nesmith, Robert I., and John S. Potter. *Treasure…How and Where to Find It.* Arco Publishing Company Inc., 1968.

Niemuth, Nyal J. *Arizona's Metallic Resources and Opportunities, 2007.* Arizona Department of Mines and Mineral Resources, Open File Report 07-24, 2007.

Patterson, Richard. *Historical Atlas of the Outlaw West.* Johnson Books, 1993.

Penfield, Thomas. *Buried Treasure in the U.S. and Where to Find It.* Grosset & Dunlap, 1969.

———. *Dig Here!* Naylor Company, 1971.

———. *A Guide to Treasure in Arizona.* True Treasure Library, 1973.

Prescott, William H. *History of the Conquest of Mexico and History of the Conquest of Peru.* Modern Library, n.d.

Probert, Thomas. *Lost Mines and Buried Treasure of the West.* University of California Press, 1977.

Ransom, Jay Ellis. *The Gold Hunter's Field Book: How and Where to Find Gold in the United States and Canada.* Harper Colophon Books, 1975.

Schurmacher, Emile C. *Lost Treasures and How to Find Them!* Paperback Library (Coronet Communications), 1968.

Steiger, Brad. *Treasure Hunting.* Ace Books Inc., 1967.

Terry, Thomas P. *United States Treasure Map Atlas.* Specialty Publishing Company, 1981.

Thomas, Alfred Barnaby. *Forgotten Frontiers: A Study of the Spanish Indian Policy of Juan Bautista de Anza, Governor of New Mexico, 1777–1787.* University of Oklahoma Press, 1969.

———. *Teodoro de Croix and the Northern Frontier of New Spain, 1776–1783: From the Original Documents in the Archives of the Indies, Seville.* University of Oklahoma Press, 1968.

Trimble, Marshall. *Roadside History of Arizona.* Mountain Press Publishing Company, 1987.

Vail, Edward L. "The Old La Cienega Stage Station Near Pantano." Available at the University of Arizona library.

Walker, Henry P., and Don Bufkin. *Historical Atlas of Arizona.* University of Oklahoma Press, 1983.

The War of the Rebellion: A Compilation of the Official Records of the Union and Confederate Armies. 128 vols. Government Printing Office, 1880–1901.

Worchester, Donald E. *The Apaches: Eagles of the Southwest.* University of Oklahoma Press, 1979.

Work Projects Administration. *Arizona: A State Guide.* Hastings House, 1940.

Young, Otis E. *Western Mining: An Informed Account of Precious-Metals Prospecting, Placering, Lode Mining and Milling on the American Frontier from Spanish Times to 1893.* University of Oklahoma Press, 1978.

Articles

Barton, Wayne. "Montezuma's Lost Treasures." *Treasure World* 7, no. 5 (April–May 1973): 28–30.

Beller, J. "Ghosts Guard the Gold." *Lost Treasure* 12, no. 4 (April 1978): 36–43.

Belli, Anthony M. "Arizona's Lost Treasure." *Lost Treasure* 36, no. 7 (July 2011): 27–30.

Black, Jack, ed. "The Baking Soda Treasure." *Best of Western Treasures Annual* (1970): 32–33, 74–75.

———. "Lost Safe of the Hassayampa." *Best of Western Treasures Annual* (1970): 6–9, 80–81.

———. "Lost Silver of Monument Valley." *Best of Western Treasures Annual* (1970): 30–31, 83–88.

———. "Secret Waybill to Arizona's El Jabonero." *Best of Western Treasures Annual* (1970): 16–19, 93–94.

———. "The Treasure of Skeleton Canyon." *Best of Western Treasures Annual* (1970): 14–15, 83–88.

Carberry, James F. "Did the Old Dutchman Leave a Big Gold Mine or Merely a Legend?" *Wall Street Journal*, October 18, 1971, 1, 23.

Carter, Sharon. "Galiruo Mystery, Yuma's Lost Treasure." *Lost Treasure* 28, no. 4 (April 2003): 21–22.

Concoles, Trini. "The Walnut Grove Flood." *Lost Treasure* 36, no. 5 (May 2011): 18.

"Desert Rat Riches." *Treasure* 10, no. 3 (April 1979): 32–34.
Dillion, George. "Apache Gold." *Gold!* 1, no. 1 (1969): 48–49, 93.
Doner, M.J. "Where Is It?" *Lost Treasure* 26, no. 3 (March 2001): 26–28.
Ebner, Ron. "Is There Nazi Gold Buried in Arizona?" *Lost Treasure* 36, no. 7 (July 2011): 60–62.
Evans, Tim. "Murdered Heiress, Missing Millions on Enduring Indiana Mystery." *Indianapolis Star*, September 22, 2015.
Ferguson, Jeff. "Lost Cave of Gold." *True Treasure* 8, no. 8 (July–August 1974): 41.
Gaines, W. Craig. "Knights of the Golden Circle Treasure." *Lost Treasure* 38, no. 9 (September 2013): 18–19.
———. "Lost Squaw Hollow Mine." *Treasure Cache* (2003): 41–42.
———. "Major Peeples' Lost Mine." *Lost Treasure* 26, no. 11 (November 2001): 16–17.
———. "Tucson's Lost Spanish Mines." *Lost Treasure* 33, no. 11 (November 2008): 16–18.
———. "The Yumas's Mines." *Lost Treasure* 32, no. 7 (July 2007): 18.
George, Viviene L. "We Had a Map to a Lost Spanish Mine." *True Treasure* 5, no. 10 (September–October 1971): 41–42, 47.
Hammond, Vern. "The 100-Year Search for the Lost Peralta." *True Treasure* 2, no. 3 (March–April 1968): 10–17.
Harrison, John. "Seventeen Fabulous Arizona Treasures." *Treasure World* 9, no. 9 (August–September 1975): 14–18.
Heald, Vern. "The Lost Bells of Tumacacori." *Western Treasures* 3, no. 5 (June 1968): 36–37.
Henson, Michael Paul. "Arizona Loaded with Ghost Towns and Treasure Sites." *Lost Treasure* 7, no. 8 (August 1982): 40–44.
———. "Treasure Hunters Enchanted by Arizona's Bounty." *Lost Treasure* 10, no. 10 (October 1985): 36–41.
Hughes, Pat. "Landslides and Lost Mines." *Lost Treasure* 26, no. 3 (March 2001): 12–13.
Ibanez, Jaime. "Waterfall Nuggets: A Cache of Gold in Grand Canyon." *Treasure Cache* (2000): 65–69.
Ives, Ronald L. "Enrique Ruhen, S.J.—Borderland Martyr." *Kiva, a Journal of the Arizona Archaeological and Historical Society* 28, no. 1 (October 1957).
Jameson, W.C. "A Man Returned from the Dead!" *Lost Treasure* 18, no. 6 (June 1993): 44–46.
Kildare, Maurice. "Did This Cowboy Find the Lost Adams Diggings?" *True Treasure* 4, no. 2 (March–April 1970): 58–64.
———. "John D. Lee's Secret Mine." *True Treasure* 4, no. 2 (March–April 1970): 14–22.

———. "The Sunlit Cave's Mission Gold." *True Treasure* 6, no. 4 (March–April 1972): 22–27.

———. "Where to Look for Placer Gold in Arizona." *True Treasure* 4, no. 12 (November–December 1970): 42–48, 53.

Kutac, C. "Buried Treasure of Rancho de Las Yumas." *True Treasure* 8, no. 12 (November–December 1974): 21.

———. "Treasure at Yuma Crossing." *True Treasure* 8, no. 6 (May–June 1974): 63–64.

"Lost Mines of Arizona." *True Frontier Treasure*, Special Issue, no. 12 (Spring 1975): 23.

Lucas, L. "Stoneman Lake Loot." *True Treasure* 8, no. 4 (March–April 1974): 66.

Masters, Al. "Arizona's Incredible Million Dollar Treasure Pit." *Saga's Treasure Special* 1, no. 1 (n.d.): 8–11, 66–69.

———. "Arizona Train Robbers' Colossal Cave Cache." *Lost Treasure* 1, no. 10 (September 1976): 16–18.

———. "Great Lost Treasure of Fort Huachuca." *Treasure World* 7, no. 1 (December–January 1973): 33–36.

McCoy, James. "The Old Indian's Tale, Spanish Gold in the Baboquivaris." *Treasure Cache* (1999): 46–49.

Meis, Joe. "The Lost Sopori Spanish Mine." *Lost Treasure* 37, no. 2 (February 2012): 27–28.

Miller, Robert H. "Lost Gold of Bicuner." *Treasure World* 6, no. 5 (April–May 1972): 15–16 and 18.

Mulkey, James E. "Apache Gold!" *Lost Treasure* 19, no. 8 (August 1994): 14–17.

———. "Southwestern Gold." *Lost Treasure* 28, no. 3 (March 2004): 36–37.

———. "Vulture's Gold: A Lost Vein of Rich Gold Ore." *Lost Treasure* 18, no. 6 (June 1993): 47–48, 50–51.

Mulkey, James E., Jr. "Gold in Bronco Canyon, Two Prospectors Discover Rich Gold Ore." *Treasure Cache* (2006): 6–8.

———. "Who's Minding the Mint?" *Lost Treasure* 21, no. 1 (January 1996): 23–25.

Penfield, Thomas. "Treasure of the Yuma Ferrymen." *True Treasure* 4, no. 6 (May–June 1970): 15–21.

Roberts, Jason (aka W. Craig Gaines). "Sycamore Canyon Gold." *Treasure Cache* (2007): 31–32.

Rose, Milton F. "The Lost Six-Shooter Mine." *Gold!* 3, no. 1 (1971): 64–66.

Sikorsky, Robert. "So Where Is the Lost Dutchman Gold?" *Lost Treasure* 10, no. 10 (October 1985): 30–33.

Stevens, Roy E. "Treasures of Sycamore Canyon." *True Treasure* 2, no. 5 (July–August1968): 23–25.

Stevenson, Roy E. "The Lost Dutchman Mine: A Mining Ghost Town and the Superstition Mountains, Part I." *Lost Treasure* 30, no. 9 (September 2013): 8–11.

Stewart, Charles. "The Great Dobie Train Robbery." *Best of Western Treasures Annual* (1970): 54, 92.

Taylor, Frank. "Dissecting the Myth of Tumacacori." *Western Treasures* 5, no. 4 (August 1970): 22–25.

Tinsman, Draco (aka W. Craig Gaines). "Montezuma's Treasures." *Treasure Cache* (2017): 32–39.

Townley, John M. "Another Lost Dutchman Mine." *Treasure World* 6, no. 1 (December–January 1972): 26–30.

———. "Rabbit Tail's Missing Mine." *True Treasure* 6, no. 6 (May–June 1972): 34–38.

Traywick, Ben T. "Yavapai County's Apache Gold." *Treasure Search* 11, no. 6 (December 1983): 26–27.

Trimble, Marshall. "The Massacre at Skeleton and Guadalupe Canyons." *True West*, blog, November 29, 2018. turewestmagazine.com.

Vannoy, Vernon. "Buried Treasure Arivaca." *Lost Treasure* 2, no. 7 (June 1977): 40.

Wagner, Ken. "Arizona Treasure." *True Frontier Special*, no. 12 (Spring 1975): 20–23, 48.

Wilson, Harold. "Lost Dutchman—The Mine that Never Was!" *Treasure World* 3, no. 2 (June–July 1969): 8, 10–11.

Wilson, Steve. "The Fabulous Lost Adams Diggings." *True Treasure* 2, no. 5 (July–August 1968): 11–22.

Websites

arizonagoldprospectors.org.

azas.arizona.edu.

azct.org.

fortwiki.com.

legendsofamerica.com.

lostadams.com.

repository.arizona.edu (for publications of Arizona Geological Survey).

westernmininghisotry.com.

wikipedia.com.

ABOUT THE AUTHOR

The author as a five-year-old cowboy.

W. Craig Gaines is the author of *Civil War Gold and Other Lost Treasure (Revised Edition)*; *Hispanic Treasures of the Eastern United States*; *Hispanic Treasures of the Western United States*; *The Confederate Cherokees: John Drew's Regiment of Mounted Rifles*; *Encyclopedia of Civil War Shipwrecks*; *Civil War Gold and Other Lost Treasures*; *Success in Life: 401 Encouraging Thoughts*; *Nostradamus' Curse*; *Great Lost Treasure Never Found*; and other books and articles. His books *Lost Oklahoma Treasure*, *Lost Texas Treasure*, *Lost California Treasure* and *Lost Missouri Treasure* were published by The History Press. Craig has been interested in lost treasure since seeing the film *Treasure Island* when he was very young. He has written lost treasure stories for a variety of treasure hunting magazines over the years. Craig is an engineer, geologist and writer. He resides with his wife, Arla, in Tulsa, Oklahoma.